STRAIGHT TALK ABOUT FRANCHSING: WHAT I LEARNED AND YOU NEED TO KNOW

A Comprehensive Guide to Making a Choice and Putting It Into Action

Cynthia Readnower

I have tried to recreate events, locales and conversations from my memories of them. In order to maintain anonymity in some instances, I have changed the names of individuals or I may have changed some identifying characteristics and details. I have expressed my opinion in this book and my perception about my experience. They may not necessarily be the opinions of others. This book contains information that might be dated and is intended only to educate and entertain. The author and publisher shall have no liability or responsibility to any person or entity regarding any loss or damage incurred, or alleged to have incurred, directly or indirectly, by the information contained in this book. You hereby agree to be bound by this disclaimer.

STRAIGHT TALK ABOUT FRANCHISING: WHAT I LEARNED AND YOU NEED TO KNOW
Cynthia Readnower

Published by Skinny Leopard Media, Bradenton, FL

ISBN: 978-0-9899893-4-3

DEDICATION

To my sons who worked alongside me in my business, to all the hard work they did, for the fun and laughter they brought, for all the memories. Thank you for being there. I love you.

TABLE OF CONTENTS

V. Human Resources

VIII. Operations

Infographics/Supporting Documents

ABOUT THIS BOOK

My experience has been in the franchise restaurant industry, owning two locations of the same franchise. They were bakery cafes. Both were over 4000 square feet and the first location ranked in the top ten franchises in sales out of over 200 in the chain. The second location struggled as the surrounding neighborhood area never achieved its predicted success and the shopping center was never fully occupied.

I've known success and I've known what it means to fight for survival. I had no prior experience in the restaurant industry but had an M.B.A. and an entrepreneurial spirit. I did all of my own accounting, marketing, and planning and worked daily in the businesses. I had general managers and managers. Some of them were awesome and some of them failed to step up to the plate. I learned a lot. I suffered a lot. I enjoyed small victories.

Although this book mentions lots of situations in the fast casual segment of the restaurant industry, the principles can be applied to all types of franchises. Franchises have lots of similarities and restaurant franchises make up the largest segment of the franchise industry as a whole. Many of the statements in this book are my opinion based on the business that I was involved in. Perhaps your experience will be different, but I hope to make you aware of real life situations and be prepared for them.

In the sections that say, "Let me tell you more…," I use specific examples that occurred in my tenure. For six years, the franchise world was my daily life. I threw myself into it whole-heartedly. I hope that my knowledge will help you make a more informed decision as to whether franchising is right for you.

INTRODUCTION

Franchising is like buying a "business in a box." You open up the box and out pops a ready-made business with systems, products and marketing materials. Your business may be successful immediately because people already know what you sell and who you are and flock to buy your product. Think "McDonald's" where you instantly know all about the food, the building and even the restrooms. You may not need experience in the franchisor's industry or perhaps even in business itself. If you have money to invest, the time to train and the ability to get financing, then that may be all it takes and you could be a business owner!

Franchises provide you with brand recognition, training, operational support, ongoing marketing support, help with choosing a location and negotiating a lease (if you have a brick and mortar location), as well as provide support for all those unexpected issues that happen in the course of doing business. Did a rat just climb out of the sewer drain and start running around your restaurant? Did the forecast for a hurricane just mean your business is forecasted to be in the eye of the storm? Did a bunch of con artists just try to rip off one of your cashiers? These types of issues do occur, albeit rarely, and a good franchisor can provide guidance (they will be careful to steer you to a lawyer if it involves legal issues) and be a calm voice in a storm. If they have a lot of franchises, they've probably already heard it all before.

Franchising can alleviate a lot of risk. Perhaps you strongly feel the urge to be your own boss. You could take a few years to research the industry trends, develop a product or set up your own business, however, by purchasing a franchise your timeline just got shorter. You have a ready-made product, you will be presented with the company's sales and success in the industry and you will have lots of help in every area of the business. It's like having someone hold your hand in every phase of the startup and operations.

Most franchisors will have many lists for you to adhere to:
1. What you need to carry in inventory (i.e. products)
2. Approved architects and builders
3. Equipment you need to purchase
4. The employees you will need
5. Décor finishing details

You'll also get lists of what marketing materials are required and how you will advertise, and perhaps even lists of job descriptions for every employee you hire, as well as how to maintain your equipment and building. When you advertise on your own (locally), it is well worth the time to learn to design your own ads (unless the franchise requires you to use theirs). Every time you place a new ad, you will usually be charged a design fee by the media. If you have to pay $75 additional for each new ad, it can really mount up. By learning to do your own, or have an employee do it for you if you have someone good at graphic arts, then it is an easy thing to just send an electronic file to the publisher of the magazine, newspaper, etc. You need to be aware of the image resolution needed and the size of the ad.

A franchisor will charge you a fee for the right to use their system, called a ***franchise fee***. The fee may have to be renewed after a certain period of time, often ten years. They will also charge you a percentage of everything you sell, called ***royalties***, and are usually paid weekly for the previous week. In addition, you may be required to buy all your equipment and fixtures from the franchisor, products, marketing materials, signage, posters, and other items, giving them the ability to make more profit off of everything they sell to you.

In return, you should have the assurance that all products you receive are quality assured, there is a training program for you and your management, you have a distribution schedule to receive inventory, you have a business consultant who will help you open your business and be available for questions and visits, you may also have a marketing specialist who helps you with advertising campaigns or groups franchisees together to buy media ads, you have the assurance that the company is constantly doing research and development for new products and stays up to date on industry trends, and you have a tried and true system that works for both you, your customers and the franchisor. They should know whom your competitors are and have a strategy for dealing with them and making sure you come out on top.

But wait, what if the franchisor doesn't stay up to date on trends, or has a personal crisis or just doesn't like you? What then? Did you just make one of the biggest investments in your life only to find a huge red flag? What if the franchisor lets another location open very close to you so you lose a lot of your business? What if they decide you must offer a product that you just know is not going to sell? What happens if they start to lose their franchisees and the whole system tanks? How are you going to recover? How are you going to keep your business going in spite of the odds?

Franchises can be great and franchises can stink. This book isn't meant to steer you either which way in making a decision but it *is* a cautionary tale of what you should consider and look out for. Nothing is guaranteed in life and business carries risk. The following just may help you make a big decision or at the very least, know what to look out for when making a choice of, "To Franchise or Not to Franchise!"

Terminology

Franchise – The actual "unit" of business purchased and operated as an extension or franchise of the business.

Franchisor – Refers to the company that offers the franchise for sale, i.e. the *seller.* For example, the corporate offices of Burger King.

Franchisee – Refers to the person or company that *purchases* one or more of the franchises.

Leasor – Refers to the company or person that owns a building or space and leases the space to someone else.

Lessee – the person or company that pays the leaseholder for the use of their building or space. This is the tenant.

THE NUTS AND BOLTS OF A BUSINESS

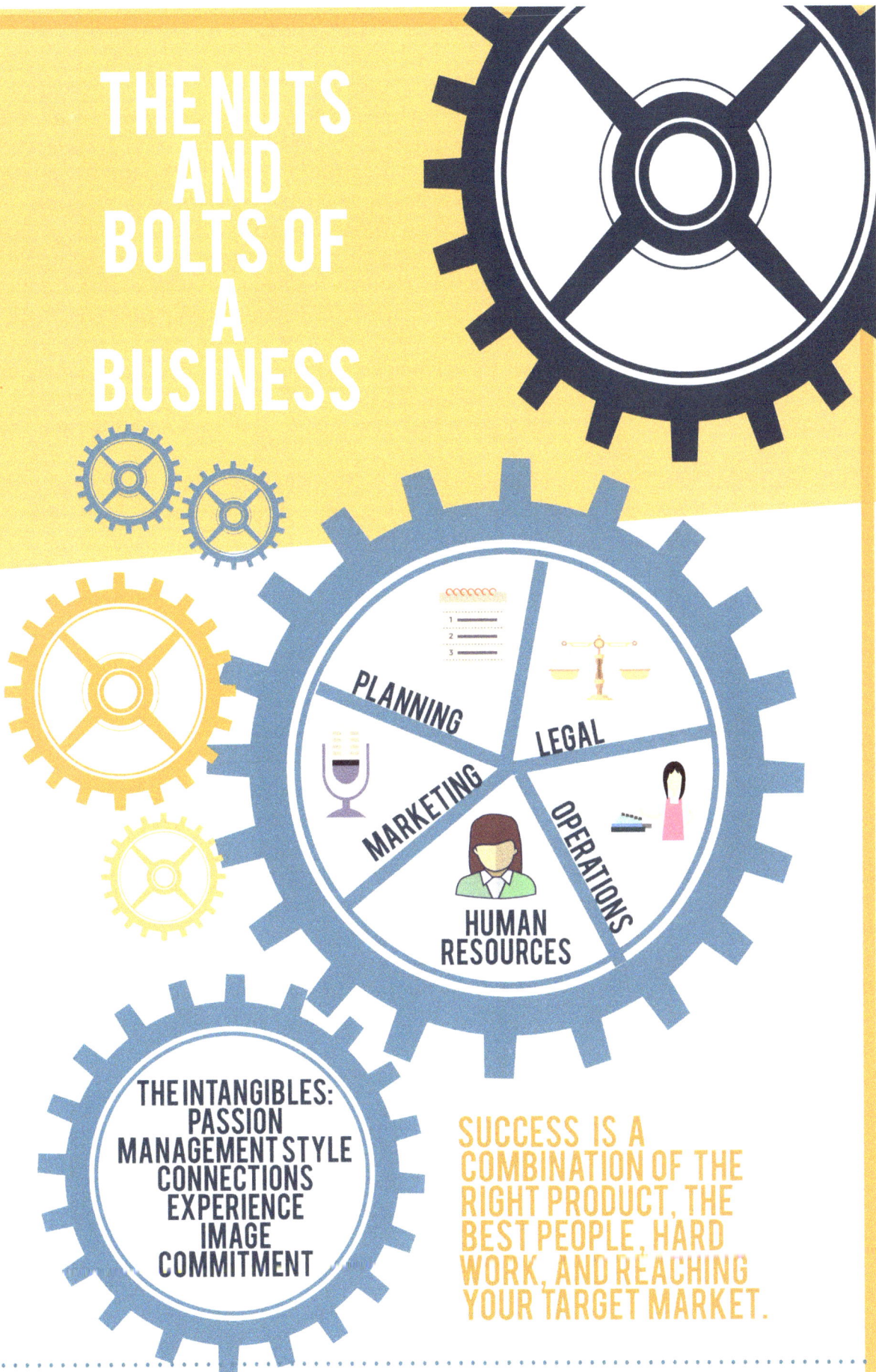

PLANNING

LEGAL

MARKETING

OPERATIONS

HUMAN RESOURCES

THE INTANGIBLES:
PASSION
MANAGEMENT STYLE
CONNECTIONS
EXPERIENCE
IMAGE
COMMITMENT

SUCCESS IS A COMBINATION OF THE RIGHT PRODUCT, THE BEST PEOPLE, HARD WORK, AND REACHING YOUR TARGET MARKET.

HOW TO MAKE A CHOICE

Are you an entrepreneur?

Many people are great business people but yet they lack the essential components to be an entrepreneur. Much of the reason has to do with risk. If you aren't willing to take risks, and that usually means with *your own* money, then you should work for someone else and let him or her absorb the risk. However, they also reap the rewards and make money off your hard work.

A very important concept to remember is that when you own your own business, you can never fully get away from it. It becomes a part of you. You *are* the business, even if you have great employees. If the business doesn't provide you with an adequate level of job and career satisfaction, then you have a problem, and one that can last for years until you can sell it or close it.

Entrepreneurs are also:

1. Confident in their abilities. They are usually very independent and don't like having people tell them what to do. They would rather figure it out on their own and enjoy problem solving. They like the creative side of coming up with a great new product, researching it and finding ways to market it.

2. They like trying new things. Some people enjoy routine but entrepreneurs thrive on change and truly want to be a part of the next big thing. They feed on the energy of "newness" and it invigorates them.

3. They enjoy a challenge. It doesn't faze them to look at a situation that seems unworkable and find a way around it. They get a lot of satisfaction of doing something other people give up on.

4. They are knowledgeable and know how to do their research. They may have a network of other associates/friends that they draw upon for ideas and/or technical information. The quest for facts and data do not deter them.

5. They enjoy a business focus. The whole world of companies, start-ups, products, inventions, creative ideas and profit are where they fit in. They feel at ease talking about it, being a part of it and living it.

6. They are strong and level headed in the midst of chaos. You never know what kind of problem you will be hit with so it pays to be calm and make even tempered decisions.

Being an entrepreneur can be a lonely business if you are the only owner of a company. You have to be a strong personality and be able to control many things and multi task continually. Of course, the upside is that you get to make all the decisions as long as they are within the franchisor's guidelines, and the downside is the same.

You may be tempted to gain a partner to even out the responsibilities but unless you are really well suited to one another, just like in a marriage, the partnership can be just as tumultuous.

"Are You An Entrepreneur?"

Challenges

Problem Solving
Trying New Things
The Unpredictable
Connecting With People
Working a Lot
Taking Risks

You Are

Confident

Knowledgeable
Business Oriented
A Good Researcher
Creative
Energetic
Level Headed

You Like

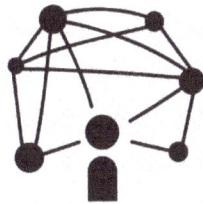

Ordinary

Being Given Orders
A 9 to 5 Job
Letting Someone Else
Reap the Rewards

You Dislike

Be Amazed

You Will

Be Proud

A look at franchising.

The excitement and anticipation of deciding to be an entrepreneur is a wonderful thing. Signing on to be a franchise can get you up and running quickly with a proven system. Being wined and dined by a company hoping to sell you a franchise can be heady, however, you must always keep in mind that tying your future, both financially and professionally to someone else requires patience, caution, and a lot of due diligence (research) on your part. Don't let the dream of being your own boss get in the way of being skeptical of everything you are told while being "courted."

When considering franchise companies ask a multitude of questions. Ask for documentation (lots of it), get the details and review the contracts for days. Write down every question and don't stop asking them until you get a good answer. You must look at the economic considerations of the present time and forecast into the future and ask questions concerning multiple scenarios. If you get any "warning bells" going off in your head or gut, step back and re-evaluate.

Do your research.

With the Internet, you have the opportunity to Google anyone and everything. Many people stop their searches within the first three pages that pop up from their query, but if you are trying to find out the gold *and* the dirt on a company, you may have to search at least ten pages deep. It is important that you know everything anyone has ever said against them so that you can make an intelligent decision - risk versus reward. Try using different search engines, too, so that you have done everything possible to find all the information available.

Find out who their officers are and Google them. What experience do they have? Have they bailed out on other companies? If a well-known chef is working for the franchisor as their research and development team and he/she chooses to leave, can he be replaced? Have there been any disputes with the company and their franchisees, suppliers, or lawsuits filed? How big is the company? Do they have adequate support staff for growth? What do their offices look like? What is the experience and education of the founders?

Most court records are now online and you can check any county for records of lawsuits. You can use all sorts of apps and websites that do investigative work and give you a report about a founder or officer. Check with the Better Business Bureau to see if any complaints are filed. Do your homework upfront and you will get a feel for the legitimacy of the company.

The franchisor usually has several of its successful franchisees willing to talk to prospects and they will likely give a positive report, however, walk into other franchises or call and ask to speak confidentially about the franchisor. You may be able to tell just as much from what they don't say as from what they do say. Few people will share their financial information with you but they will likely let you know if they are disgruntled. Offer to meet them on neutral ground, away from their business so that they may speak freely and not have to put on a positive face. Be respectful and let them know what a favor they are doing by speaking with you. Most will enjoy being in the position to share their success or their burdens.

Are they rock solid?

The stability of a franchisor may be hard to judge. There could be many things going on behind the scenes that you will never know about. What if one of the officers is getting a divorce and he is being sued for his piece of the business? What if one of the founders is arrested in another country and placed on house arrest for months (yes, it happened)? Are they closing franchises? How many are they opening at once and will that tax their support operations? What suppliers do they have contracts with? Is there anything going on in the world that could affect their product or support? When gas prices go up, then many companies add a fuel surcharge to deliveries outside a certain area. Are their products heavily dependent on deliveries?

What if green onions are found to be responsible for an outbreak of food poisoning or worse in multiple states and someone gets sick after eating at the franchise? That is just what happened to Chi Chi's Mexican Restaurants in 2003 when three people died and 500 were sickened after contracting Hepatitis A from the onions. One mistake like that can ruin the entire system. Some things just can't be anticipated but you should look at the systems in place with the franchisor, their back up plans, and your own control over the most likely situations. Again... what is the risk versus reward?

Stability doesn't just include the company but also its product or the technology, the economy, the city you want to open the franchise in, and every possible piece of the environment that could affect you.

Sophisticated decision skills?

Are they located in a major city that has different market segments than yours, can they make the right decisions regarding products to market them to a smaller city? The location of a franchise does make a difference. Depending on what type of industry it is, whether the company is progressive or conservative based on the part of the country/city they are located in, *will* affect research and development. If they have locations in small towns, will they create trendy products? Probably not. They may want to walk the middle of the road. If their major markets are bigger cities, then will the products fit into Smalltown, U.S.A.?

Different parts of the country have different cultural values that can affect company policies. If the company is in the Midwest, will it value family and not have people staffing their support hotlines on the weekends? If they are in the more religious South, will they close on Sundays? What holidays will they require you to stay open for?

HOW TO CHOOSE A FRANCHISE

Find a successful franchise that interests you

Count the customers

Visit several locations

What are customers buying?

Multiply the number of customers times the amount of their estimated purchases. How much money is the franchise taking in?

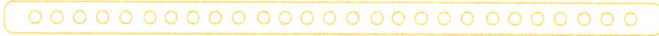

Estimate their monthly sales

Estimate their costs: fixed and variable

Are the costs in line with sales? Can you make a profit? Is it attractive enough to move forward?

Talk to the franchisor

Here are ten other areas to consider when looking at a franchise:

1. Privately held company versus public company.

Privately held companies (which the majority of franchise companies are) do not have to reveal financial statements to the general public. The private sector (i.e. *not* featured on any stock exchange) does not have to reveal information or answer to a *public* board of directors regarding strategies or decisions. If you truly want to know what type of profit a private corporation is making, you will not know unless the company *wants* you to know. If the franchise corporation is private, you may never know if they are financially solvent or not. You may not know just how much profit they are making off of their franchisees and whether it seems "fair" to you. Although a private corporation is good in that it doesn't have to answer to the public, it also doesn't have to answer to *you*.

In a private corporation, if the owner dies or is ill, the stability of the company may be in danger. It depends on the successors *or* a board of directors who have been appointed by the owners, as to who is able to fill in the position.

If the corporation is public, then records can be accessed by shareowners and the financial information is published in an annual report. Public companies (those traded on a stock exchange) have to make their information available so that their shareholders can decide if they are doing the right thing. Before a franchising operation becomes big enough and successful enough to attract lots of attention, it is usually operated by the startup owner(s) as a privately held company. This means that if the owner lacks common sense or business sense, the *franchisee* (you) will not be informed of the consequences of those decisions.

Every decision made by the *franchisor* affects your income and success. So, just because it seems logical that the franchisor would be interested in the franchisee's success, i.e. your success means more royalties, often the business decisions depend on other things. For example, marketing decisions for new products or operations may be made based on the experiences of the owner. If the owner just got back from Italy and loved the food, will they want to introduce an Italian flair into your offerings? If the company is private, they do not have to incur the wrath of shareholders and can often get away with making less logical decisions than if they have to explain themselves.

If you require a more diverse product line or services because of stiffer competition in your geographic area, then you may suffer at the decisions of the owners. If certain marketing promotions are covered in your royalty fees, the owners may decide to cut back on promotional materials or advertising to save money. A publicly held company must answer to its stockholders and a board of directors, which will, hopefully, keep their decisions more reasonable. A privately held company, where the owners control everything, does not have to answer to anyone.

GNC, Hyatt Hotels, Noodles & Company, Potbelly Sandwich Shop, RE/MAX, Dunkin Brands and McDonalds are examples of publically held companies. They have stockholders and the stockholders expect dividends and some of the profit is distributed through those dividends. The companies also had to pay hefty fees to go public through an IPO (initial public offering). Most companies that go with an IPO are usually looking to pay down their debt, expand or acquire a second brand.

2. Purchasing power.

Some franchises require that all products be purchased directly from them. If they are not very large, or if they don't pull enough weight in their industry, then they may not have much room for bargaining with the wholesale suppliers that sell them the raw goods and your costs may be higher than desired. Purchasing power often equates to size. The larger the order, the bigger the discount. Is the franchisor large enough to draw the discounts or is it part of a cooperative that buys in bulk? Do they have contracts with large players or do they depend on regional suppliers that may or may not provide good service and supply?

If there is allowance for you to find your products on the open market or at least a good portion of them, you have more freedom to control your costs. If the parent company supplies all your products, what happens if they have an equipment failure and there is no other source of supply? For example, perhaps they produce your supply of proprietary tortilla chips and their equipment fails. It sets their production back for three days so when the delivery truck leaves for your location, they only send you ten cases instead of twenty. What are your options to fulfill your own customer demand?

Any logo items will likely require purchase from the franchisor. They will have a large contract with a supplier to put the logo on any merchandise and then it is marked up and sold to the franchisee. This can include cups, napkins, T-shirts, aprons, etc.

When the market has a shortage of an item, say pumpkins get root rot and the crop doesn't produce, who gets the bulk of the crop to be able to fulfill the special recipe for pumpkin muffins? Also, the distance that the franchisee is from the supplier may mean higher delivery charges.

3. Equipment purchases.

If the franchisor has specified certain vendors or certain brands, the franchisor *may* be receiving "special deals" from the supplier for everything they sell, or if the franchisor owns "corporate" locations that also need the equipment, they may receive a large discount. This leads to inferior equipment choices and may hurt the franchisee. Most franchisors will require that you purchase your startup equipment from them as well as replacement equipment. Sometimes, the equipment is sub par and you will pay for it in equipment failures or in replacement costs. Replacement costs may be much higher purchasing from the franchisor rather than on the open market.

Once you own the equipment, it is up to you to maintain it and fix it. If the owners have selected a piece of equipment that wasn't meant for the job, it becomes your problem. In my experience, although the franchisor knew the high failure rate and high cost of replacement of a particular piece of equipment, they failed to find a replacement or refine the operations so that the franchisee would be relieved of the burden of constant repair in spite of numerous franchisees asking for change. Another consideration is about how critical a piece of equipment is for sales of certain products. If you can't do without it and there is a high failure rate, you may need a spare to see you through the downtime. This adds to your costs.

What is the cost to your business to tell a customer a certain product is not available? How much time does it take to repair? Can you repair it yourself or does it need a specialist? Where does the serviceman come from? Do you have to pay for his travel time? What is the downtime? ? Do you have a maintenance agreement, what cost is the agreement?

Many franchises will insist you purchase a software system that they have tested and used for their business. This can apply to a point of sale system and also an accounting system. If they require that you submit financial reports as a part of the franchise agreement, then standardized reports make sense. It also gives you some insurance that you know the software works and is at a certain level of standards.

On the negative side is that you may have to purchase a software system that is more than you need, requires higher than normal maintenance fees or is not a locally based company that can assist you when you need help. A poor decision on the franchisor's part will impact your business.

Just as in any type of business, the solidness of the company, their pricing, the support you receive and their longevity in business as well as their level of customer service should all be investigated.

⚜ ⚜ ⚜

Let me tell you more...

I had to replace the tires on my car and visited a franchised tire store. I noticed that they had difficulty pulling up my records (I had used them before but the systems weren't interactive) and then they printed a quote out on an old dot matrix printer (slow and cumbersome which should have been dumped years ago). I asked about it, curious as to why they would still be using something so outdated. The manager explained that because any new equipment must be purchased through the franchisor at a cost of $40,000, it would cut into their profits too much to allow them to purchase newer technology. Their computer systems were not interactive and processing time for a customer was poor.

⚜ ⚜ ⚜

4. Independent Association of Franchisees.

Most franchises will have established, through several of the franchisees, an independent association of the individually owned locations. Every franchise needs an association that is totally independent of the franchisor. *It should:* be a place to exchange information, solve problems, develop buying cooperatives, have legal counsel, air gripes, create back up plans if the franchisor should have problems such as financial issues, i.e. the death of an owner, arrests of owners, bankruptcy, going out of business, etc. Being able to create connections with other franchise owners is IMPORTANT! This group might also discuss issues concerning operations, sales, and marketing as well as feed requests and information to the franchisor. The stronger the association, the more pressure that can be put on the franchisor to change operations or to listen to issues.

Most associations will have a lawyer on call to advise them of their rights when dealing with the owners. It is advantageous for both the franchisor and the franchisee to have a strong participation. United, a group can negotiate purchasing power, solve problems and plan for the future. Unfortunately, some franchisors are threatened by a strong association and may work against it. I have seen franchisees that attempted to start an association targeted with unannounced inspections, warnings for ridiculous things, and intimidated into renouncing their leadership or membership.

5. Franchise Disclosure Document or Universal Franchise Offering Circular.

The UFOC (Universal Franchise Offering Circular), now named the FDD (Franchise Disclosure Document) is one of those things that is extremely helpful and also very annoying. It can be the size of a book and take hours to read. This document, required by law to be issued by the franchising parent corporation lists any lawsuits pending against a corporation, bankruptcies, trademarks, restrictions, fees, obligations of the company, contracts and more. Although reading this document can be likened to watching paint dry, it is essential reading. Be sure to question everything! Lawsuits against the company or initiated by the company should be red flags. While there are often times that litigation is necessary, it should only be a last resort. Research each one and see if there is a common thread. Obviously, anyone can sue anyone in our society, but more than one or two lawsuits should make you wary.

A franchise organization will most likely have a lawyer on staff. If so, that also means that the franchisor has level legal costs, whether they are involved in many lawsuits or not. Beware of the type of lawyer they have and how many suits they are involved with. This makes it easier to sue or use the possibility of a lawsuit against a franchisee since they don't have to pay the additional costs of hiring an outside lawyer.

If the FDD/UFOC looks like a book, is the company trying to confuse you with their legal-ease? Having to pay an attorney to read an inch thick document could cost you some big bucks but it is essential to be aware of what's in it. Try reading through it yourself and then ask the franchisor to explain anything you do not understand. Get clarifications in writing if you can although the franchisor may be leery of doing that. The FDD is also protection for the company.

Other items that should be included in the document are any bankruptcies the franchisor has had, the franchise fee, other fees, restrictions, renewals, terminations, transfers, proprietary information, the company's business experience, source of products, trademarks, patents, copyrights, ways disputes are settled (usually by mediation), obligations, and sometimes other items such as how much money you can earn. Your individual contract should include and spell out your territory, receipt of monies, any financing through the franchisor, and other things such as your obligation to actually manage or be involved in the business daily.

6. Inspections.

The franchisor should and will make inspections of all franchises. This is to every franchise location's benefit because one customer's experience elsewhere affects whether they purchase from *your* location or not in our mobile society. Usually, this is performed by a "franchise consultant" or "business consultant, a person assigned to territories that visits the location and then makes a report. Sometimes, they are unannounced so that the consultant can see the real operation and not just a "show".

My experience has been more negative than positive with the consultants. Inspections lasting for two days, seeing a new consultant every few months to a year so that there is no rapport or relationship, inspection reports of fourteen pages or more, and consultants that don't even understand the operations can be very frustrating and hindering. A good consultant should work with you to solve problems, streamline operations, and ensure quality control. They should use their experience in the industry to educate you and be your partner.

7. Legal representation.

Some franchisors will have you work with a recommended lawyer to negotiate your lease and check over documents. Beware, you should never allow any lawyer to manage anything without your complete and full understanding. You must use common sense and read all documents yourself, ten times if necessary, to question every clause and every negotiation. You must not be intimidated by legal speak. You will have to live with the results for years to come. You have very little recourse against a mistake. I was told that trash removal was included in my lease by my attorney. Two years later, I was invoiced for thousands of dollars by the landlord for past waste removal. After having to hire another attorney to review my lease, I was told it was "silent" on the matter, which meant it could go either way. In another instance, a clause for reduced rent based on the occupancy of the shopping center was phrased incorrectly, to my detriment, although my attorney told me he was "100% sure" of his interpretation. Once he realized he was incorrect, he stopped taking my phone calls.

8. The numbers.

Of course, the franchisor is there to sell more franchises. They make their money on selling franchises, royalties on your sales, markups on equipment and products, and also possibly on markups in distribution channels. If they own the distribution company that delivers your products, they may also charge you an additional fee for the delivery in the form of a fuel surcharge, etc. When they sell you a franchise, you have no way of knowing if the data you receive regarding the potential profit you can make is entirely correct or not. Variables can be large depending on geographic location, cost per square foot of leased space that you have to pay, liability insurance, wildly fluctuating impact fees, your loan interest, utility costs, and employee costs. In my experience, speaking to other franchise owners in the system is not a great benefit when it involves money or their profit and loss. Most want to look successful whether they *are* or *are not*, and since many businesses involve cash dealings, they won't reveal the true nature of their profit and loss lest you have connections to the IRS. Also, the costs of a company owned franchise (owned by the franchisor and operated by them) is probably less than what you can expect based on economies of scale and the fact they are supplying their own product to themselves.

Anyone can spin numbers in different ways. If you are shown any type of statistics, make sure you have no doubts about what they are saying. You might want to inquire as to what statistics are available on how many franchises have opened and closed, what the average length of opening time is from signing on to making sales, what the average sales amounts are, the average profit percentage, the number of locations in different geographical areas, how much media exposure there has been, where the advertising dollars are going and if that would benefit you in your chosen geography, the average type of customer along with their income, age, and other demographics, as well as anything else you can possibly think of.

9. The balance of power.

Every franchisor will be charming when trying to sell you a franchise. They will portray their franchise in the best light. However, once you are in their network and under contract, they may show another side and that is when, if conditions in the marketplace are tough, the franchisor may push some of the franchisees into doing things the franchisees don't want, or don't' have the money to do.

You must be aware of every detail in your franchise contract, your rights by law, and what you can and can't do. I have seen franchisees targeted by the corporation because of personality conflicts, lack of professionalism, stubbornness on either parts, and heaven knows what else. Once an adversarial relationship develops, the corporation may seek to show their power over you. One franchisee was inspected three times in a month although all reports were favorable, others have been denied shipments of proprietary products "by mistake," told that they must give the company their bank account information so that royalties could be directly withdrawn (in the day when this was not necessarily done), or that they were required to do other things because policies had changed even though the contract they signed had not. There is not much cost to the company to file a lawsuit against a franchisee if they employ a lawyer on staff. Think of it this way, that a lawyer is already on the payroll and the only thing it costs the franchisor to sue someone is the court fee.

You should also ask to see written communication that has been issued to franchises in the past year. At one point in my career, every piece of communication we received from the parent company issued the edict that if we did not do what we were being told (i.e. change a policy, change a product, etc.) we would have our franchise agreement revoked. This included having a non-approved vase of flowers or too many newspapers on our newsstand.

It is possible that when a franchisor feels like they have lost control of their franchisees due to a franchise association, or that the franchisees are refusing to do things that are "mandated," the franchisor may threaten the franchisee with taking over the franchise. Reasons are easy to fabricate, i.e. a failed inspection, failure to report in a timely manner, unpaid royalties, etc. It is important to always keep the chain of communication open and not just wait until the franchisor "targets" you. You should always make an effort to talk with the franchisor and have a healthy relationship. This may come in handy during tough times. Of course, if you always adhere to their policies this shouldn't be an issue. The more successful you are, the less likely you will be to attract the franchisor's attention, unless your success is a reason the franchisor may want their franchise back in the fold. Then, you may need to seek legal representation to fight having to give your franchise up.

10. Standards.

Any franchise that becomes successful does, in some part, by maintaining standards. They provide quality, value and excellent customer service. Different industries require more or less standardization. Certain franchises are immediately recognizable when you walk in the door based on décor. This décor usually changes with the times and that means expenses for the franchisee. Make sure your contract spells out what you will be required to update or change and the limit of your investment. It is a tragic thing to reach your five year mark, not having paid off your initial startup loan and be handed a requirement to remodel your location with a cost of $250,000 or more. Failure to do so may give the company the right to take over your location, forcing you into bankruptcy. Don't ever enter into an agreement without knowing all the details.

There are many more things to consider. Always remember to slow down, check out the details, and then proceed with caution. I would recommend working in the industry for a good six months or in a franchise location to determine if there are issues you are not aware of. Most of all, you must love the business. Look at the hours of operation, the busy times of the year, the amount of customer contact, the type of employees you will hire. All of these elements will contribute to your satisfaction, not just the income you can derive.

The following is a list of the major categories of franchises available. Some can be "work at home" types of jobs while most require an office or a specialty space. Some of the top franchises today include hotels, fitness franchises, restaurants, convenience stores, damage restoration (fire or smoke), hair salons and senior care.

Types of Franchises

Computer- repairs, instructional
Hotels
Automotive- rental agencies, car washes, car repair
Food – restaurants, candy, ice cream, frozen yogurt
Children- Instruction, drama, computers, dance, gymnastics, parties, day care
Cleaning - green
Clothing- closets, used, shoes
Decorating - window décor, interior design, lighting, mattresses
Fitness- fitness studios, gyms
Handyman business
Pet- pet washing, pet stores, pet bakery, bird food, boarding, pet spas
Printing
Real Estate brokerage
Remodeling - Re-bath, flooring, re-surfacing, tile
Retail- hobby, convenience stores
Salons
Self Storage
Services – carpet cleaning, water restoration, jewelry repair
Senior Care
Small Business- business brokers
Tax
Travel- vacation rentals, cruises, golf vacations
Restoration
Learning/Tutoring
Sports- golf, used equipment
Medical/Health- massage, weight loss
Coaching
Technology
Movers

Types of Franchises

What's Right For You?

Food and
Beverage

Senior Care

Hotels

Hair Salons

Children

Automotive

Technology

Self Storage

Pet Care

Home

Sports/ Fitness

Services

Real Estate   Handyman   Travel   Closet Design   Business Services

Let me tell you more...

Will I Get Rich?

I once had a customer walk into my business and try to find out information about how much profit I made on my franchise. He saw how busy we were but didn't have any experience in the restaurant business. He asked several question and then popped out with, "So what do you make a year, about $2 million?" And he meant profit, not sales. I was dumbfounded by his perception. If I made that much profit in a year, I would be in my villa on the French Riviera, not freshening up a customer's coffee. What he saw was a busy place but had no concept of the cost of labor, fixed and variable costs and all the things it took to keep the customers coming through the doors. Just because something appears to be a certain way, doesn't mean it is. It is easy to have blinders on and think that you will make a lot of money because you see that a business has lots of customers. There are so many things that make up the real formula for success.

Most people want to make money, that's why you go into business in the first place. However, when you buy a franchise you have to assume that because of the contracts and investment you need to be able to make money until your loans are paid back, the franchise buys you out or you sell your business. For most franchises, the contract or term of the franchise is good for ten years and most small business loans take ten years to pay back.

So assuming that you are tying yourself to this franchise for ten years, unless you can sell it early, then you need to do some soul searching which most people will avoid doing. The reason? Many people just don't want to know the negative things that can happen. They have been star struck with the first glow of owning a franchise and think they can sit back and reap the profits. Sometimes that happens, but.... the majority of the time most franchise owners will tell you they had no idea of the long hours it would take, the hard work, the difficulty dealing with employees, the problems working with the franchisor and the inability to sustain customer loyalty. It's like anything else, the glow fades over time and you are left with a daily grind, so you better make sure you are suited for this work from the get-go.

Why Buy a Franchise?

The franchisor may be a ready-made success story. Everybody knows their name.

You want someone to help you and hold your hand in starting and owning a business.

You don't have enough business or industry experience to go it alone.

You believe in their product.

Their formula works. There are many success stories.

You want to have your business up and running faster than you can start your own.

They provide you with unique tools or support.

They are one of the fastest growing franchises in the country.

You can get financing because they are a known entity. Banks will open their arms to you.

They offer you a special deal to buy multiple franchises.

There is safety in the number of franchises they have, the franchise association is strong and carries weight with the franchisor.

They can sell you everything you need in one package.

They are on the cutting edge of trends.

They provide training, at a reasonable cost or included in the franchise fee.

They have an approved list of subcontractors such as architects, attorneys, accountants, design professionals and construction companies, etc., with whom they have formed stable relationships.

They have a proprietary product that you can't get anywhere else.

They impress you by the way the company is run, their company culture, their success, etc.

Why
Buy A Franchise

- **Ready Made Success**
- **Quick Start-up**
- **Fits Your Lifestyle**
- **Cutting Edge of Trends**

You believe in them

They are growing quickly

You want support, tools and training

You can get financing

There is a franchise association for support

You get a special deal, perhaps multiple franchises

You lack confidence or experience to go it alone

They have a list of contractors, architects, design professionals, and suppliers who know their business

They have an innovative product or marketplace

Their formula works for everyone

Reasons NOT To Buy a Franchise

You are independent and don't want to be controlled by anyone. You don't enjoy having someone tell you what to do.

You are creative and will be bored by the same routine day in and day out with no room for change.

You aren't sure the franchise can make it in the long run. Have they reached the end of their run at the top?

The costs are higher than other similar franchises. They may be top dog now, but what about a few years from now?

You will lose profit to royalties. Royalties can be the make it or break it number on a profit and loss statement.

You will have to renew the franchise and pay another franchise fee after ten years and you believe you will want to own the franchise for twenty years or more.

Their contracts are not specific enough as to future requirements for remodeling and other requirements that could cost you big dollars.

They insist you sell products in your marketplace that your customers just do not want. You know your area better than they do.

They are an industry follower, not a leader. Do you want to be on the cutting edge of trends?

You have industry knowledge and can make it on your own; starting your own business and you won't have to pay royalties.

You have experience running a business and you don't need a ready-made system.

You have Googled the company and its officers and find some negative things about their past or their ethics.

They make verbal promises and won't put it in writing, preferring to deal with a handshake.

If you project ten years ahead, you don't see how the franchise will stay fresh enough to continue to bring in the profits you need or want.

You see too many things that can go wrong.

You think you won't have to work as hard at your own business as you would adhering to a franchisor's requirements.

You must invest in multiple franchises from the start and aren't a multi-millionaire.

They insist that you commit to opening a new franchise every six months or a year if you buy multiple locations.

They won't give you the territory protection that you can live with.

There are too many competitors in the field in their niche.

They are very strict on their policies and you can see conflict ahead.

You've added up all the investment costs, estimated the revenue and you just don't see the profit that they tell you the franchise makes. Trust yourself. This should not be a leap of faith for you but black and white numbers.

You've talked to other franchisees in the system and you just can't see yourself being a part of them.

You won't enjoy the work! This could be your life for the next ten years or more.

Reasons NOT To Buy A **Franchise**

You are very independent... You don't want to be controlled.

You are creative and will get bored by routine.

The franchise is at the end of their life cycle.

Their costs are higher than owning your own original business.

Consider:

They won't put promises in writing.

Contracts are too vague for future changes.

You must buy or open multiple units too quickly.

They are an industry follower, not a leader.

Royalties will eat up too much profit.

You can't get territory protection.

There is already too much competition.

Ask around

Don't do it if you just don't see the potential and the profit that the franchisor tells you that you will have! Trust yourself.

What Makes a Particular Franchise Attractive?

Low initial investment.

Lower royalties.

The opportunity to purchase products from different suppliers rather than just the franchisor. You can work deals with other suppliers.

Free training for *future* staff, not just when you open.

A unique marketing niche.

Something that you would love to do over a period of time.

Working with people you enjoy.

Having customers/clients you enjoy.

The franchise is well matched to your lifestyle.

Less risk than other options.

The opportunity to own multiple franchises and have them run by a staff so that you just oversee the whole operation and make profits.

Low building investment. The franchisor doesn't require expensive furnishings or fixtures.

No need to update your building very so often (for example if a restaurant changes its décor).

A forward thinking franchisor who stays on top of trends.

They won't nickel and dime you to death. For example, do they require uniforms? Do you automatically have to take on every new product? Do you have mandatory marketing materials that you pay for?

What Makes A Good Franchise?

Low initial investment

Lower royalties

Less risk

Free training

Future free training

Ability to train your own staff

Working with people you enjoy

Unique product or market niche

It matches your lifestyle

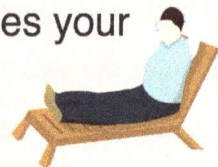

You would love it for a long time

DO YOU/THEY HAVE WHAT IT TAKES?

The honeymoon phase.

Most entrepreneurs feed off the energy of a big shiny new venture. They have plenty of enthusiasm and can work long hours to get their business open because they are so excited about it. This can last during the prospecting phase, the start up phase and then the grind sets in. All the fun they had with the creative process turns into a daily routine that never ends. Will the profit sustain you through the grind? Will you find other tasks to keep your interest? Do you need the constant stimulation of "newness?"

Most entrepreneurs start out in business with the idea that they will get the business up and running, make enough profit to hire someone else to run it, and then either retire or start a new business. Most believe that if they can get the business running smoothly there won't be as much need for them to check on every detail. That's part of the American dream, however, the reality is often different. The profit margin may not be there to enable you to hire someone at the salary needed for them to run the business for you. The economy may not support that extra salary either when times are tough. And if the economy is booming, you will have to compete with everyone else for labor and end up paying higher wages. Just remember that you may be running the business yourself for longer than expected.

Can you do this for ten years?

Owning a franchise is not just about a business, but it is also a lifestyle. Multiple factors need to be considered such as personal satisfaction, the time you are able to take away from the business, the types of people who will work for you, the types of people who will be your customers, how many hours it will take to run the business, whether it is appropriate to bring your family into the business, if your children would be safe and comfortable there and not disruptive, and a host of other considerations just as individual as you are.

At this time, some of the most profitable franchises are related to "elder homecare." That means you have to deal with worried family members; find trustworthy, patient employees with some type of medical training, schedule; be able to make the elderly comfortable with your company, and generally be a people person. If that's *not* you, then don't let the attractive profit potential sway you. For the long haul and your sanity, you must find a match between your interests, the way you want to work, the risk you are willing to take and the future you want to have. Will you still find the satisfaction in going to work?

It's great to have a system in place for your business that the franchisor has already proven to work, however boredom can be a problem. Most people want the ability to at least be a little creative.

Especially if you plan on being a part of the business on a daily basis, how much creativity to you need in your life? The more set the routine, the less give and take there is to do things differently. Perhaps just having different customers will give you the feeling that each day is not the same, but perhaps not. Just how many times can you clean an espresso machine and not begin to resent it?

Is it all about profit or is it also about job satisfaction? When you decide to open a franchise, you need to decide if this is going to be "strictly business" or is it a place you will spend a lot of time in. Even if it is *just* business, you will still have to deal with people and that means interactions with employees, even if you can afford to have someone else run the day to day operations. You will still have to know the complete ins and outs of the business, since your "general manager" may get sick, walk out or take off. No one is exempt from life's unexpected events.

When choosing a franchise or business that you will be involved in daily, don't just consider the here and now as to how enthusiastic you are about the whole thing. Think of the future; five years from now, ten years from now; will you still be as enthusiastic? Will you still have the urge to get out of bed in the morning and go to work? The work you choose must be intellectually satisfying and emotionally fulfilling to go the distance.

Once you believe that the business will keep you interested, then break down the parts such as accounting, sales, marketing, human resources and hiring/firing to see if you can manage every piece or what type of employee and expertise you will need to hire to manage that part. Does it still fit in with your business model? Can you find the help you need at a manageable cost? Will this fit into your long-term goals?

Does it feel right?

Unfortunately, sometimes the hottest franchises are the newest. Wealthy business people may be able to plunk down millions of dollars to buy out all the franchises in one particular state. If you only want one or maybe even four, you may not get approved because a franchisor will most likely go with the big money. It makes sense to them to have fewer owners and ones that they know are already successful. You must take a leap off the deep end to sign on early enough to secure a territory and sometimes it's just a gut feeling. When a franchise is suddenly featured in *Inc. Magazine* or named a top ten franchise, then you might have to jump on the bandwagon and take a chance, but that chance comes with increased risk. If the company hasn't been around long enough to judge its track record, how do you know it will still be here ten years from now? You don't!

The Franchise System

The Basics

What you can expect

#1

Q Paying Royalties

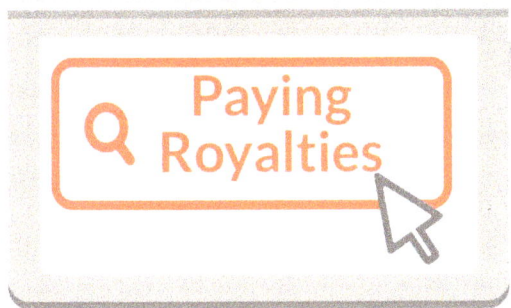

You pay 5-10% of your sales dollars to use their system

#2

⬆ **A System**
⬇ **Conformity**

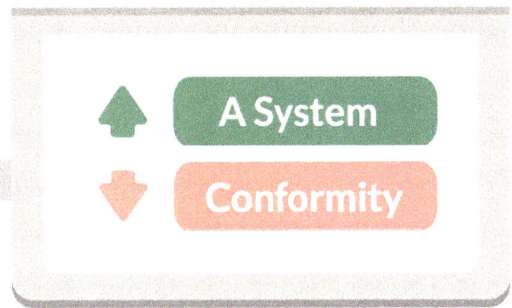

A system kickstarts your business but conformity doesn't allow for creativity

#3

Economies of scale

The franchisor should be able to purchase items more cheaply

The nuts and bolts of a ready made business

#4

Training

Training is the cornerstone of your business

Potential for faster profits

You're buying their experience

The franchise consultant/ business consultant.

Franchisors have a team that helps you get your franchise off the ground. Hopefully, the team has industry experience and can truly enlighten you when you need some sound advice. You want seasoned veterans who have been down this road before and can give you quick fixes, see a problem before it happens and guide you to the easiest opening ever as well as be there for the long haul.

The business or franchise consultant helps you open your franchise. This key person will be assigned territories and make rounds of the franchisees to offer new information, help them train, do inspections and make sure that the franchise is being run in accordance with their regulations, policies and procedures. Hopefully, this person has been in the industry a long time and knows the competition, the pitfalls and what to do in any situation. Ideally, this should be the "go to" person you call when you find out that a competitor is opening down the street or if a piece of equipment fails and you need to find a repairman quickly.

The consultant should be a support person but can also be adversarial if their main function is only to inspect you and provide feedback to the franchisor. Do they use consultants that know the industry? How much industry background do they have? Do they have management, ownership and operational experience?

Some companies will also have a marketing consultant in addition to a franchise consultant. The marketing consultant's function is to work with advertising, marketing plans, and the media to help promote your franchise. Often, a portion of the advertising is done in regional or national blocks and then you are also responsible for spending a certain percentage yourself locally on promotions. The marketing consultant should have knowledge of the industry as well as being familiar with the costs of television, radio and print ads, promotions such as price specials, coupons and other ways to pull in business. They should be aware of what has worked for other franchisees as well as what the competition is doing.

⚜ ⚜ ⚜

Let me tell you more...

Most of the business/marketing consultants that the franchisor sent were really smart, experienced and great people. Once in a while, a new one would come along and make life hell. One business consultant entered my restaurant and in the first conversation told me, "I can shut you down." It was interesting that this man walked into a top ten store in sales and started with threats instead of, "How can I help you?" Shocked and angry, this started months of constant aggravation and having to prove to him that we adhered to all policies and procedures as set by the franchisor. Many of us complained to the franchisor and eventually, the business consultant moved on. It was something that should never have happened but which we franchisees had no control over.

⚜ ⚜ ⚜

Will they compete with themselves?

Does the franchisor have other franchises that will compete with yours or be complementary? Are their resources stretched too thin? Will their attention be pulled away from focusing on *your* franchise?

The franchisor may decide that after having 200 successful franchises open, that they want to change or expand their product line. Perhaps, instead of offering twenty products, they now want to offer thirty, but your franchise cannot expand due to whatever restraints there may be. So, now the newer franchises offer a wider product line and you are still stuck with the original offering. Could this happen? Could you end up competing with a newer franchise that's only fifteen minutes away from you?

The franchisor, by their very nature, needs to be creative. What happens to you if the people at the top get a little bored and create a new concept? Will they pull resources from the original franchise? Will you be left in a lurch? Will there be pressure for you to buy into the new franchise idea? Will the new concept share the same support network of business consultants, marketing professionals, product delivery system, etc.?

Conforming to all the others.

How strict are they with insisting that every franchise is exactly alike or is there freedom for individuality? Most franchise owners will agree that they know their marketplace better than the franchisor ever could. An owner may work in the business daily, know the customers personally and/or may have lived in the location all their lives. The franchisee may realize that their own location needs lower/higher prices, a more friendly/sophisticated appearance, more/less freebies, less product inventory for that seasonal product that just doesn't go over well in their town.

Will you have to share the exact same holidays, be open the exact same hours or have the exact same uniform/building/décor/product line, etc. as everyone else.

There are some benefits to consumers for having every franchise be exactly the same. Customers know what to expect and the respect and patronage they feel for other locations will translate to yours. However, if your town is known for something special and tourists are drawn to your town for that product and *you* don't offer it, then "ouch." Think lobster bisque in New England or barbeque in Memphis.

How tough is the franchisor on requirements? How frequently do they change requirements? How durable are the uniforms? What about hair requirements? Facial hair requirements?

Most franchisors have a certain style that they will want you to maintain. Is the company trendy or conservative? Do they allow visible tattoos? What about body piercings? They may specify how they want your employees to look. Will this work in your town? Do they change with the times?

Risk versus reward.

No one wants to plan for anything negative when just starting out in business. But how probable is it for the economy to tank, for oil prices to rise so that discretionary spending is cut back and how recession proof is your product? If you buy your franchise when the economy is booming, then what effects would an economy downturn have? Some franchises may do even better, but look at your expected profit margin and see if you can live with less. If margins are very tight, then perhaps this is not the best franchise for you.

An up and coming franchise entails more risk. A franchise that has been around long term may be at the end of their life cycle. Are they innovative, do they conduct research and development, what is their reputation in new ideas and trends?

It's exciting to be a part of a new franchise that is taking the world by storm. Fast forward five or ten years, and the concept may no longer be on fire. Is the franchisor continually researching for new and better ways? Even if they tell you that it is their policy to do so, what happens if they lose the driving force of their research? What changes will be made so that you have to carry new products? What assurances do you have? Can you survive if lots of competitors move in nearby?

The life cycle of any product is normally shaped like a bell curve. It starts to take off, reaches a peak, stays there for a certain amount of time and then starts to decline, unless injected with new products or new life. Are you buying in at the peak or where the product is on a decline? Although you are not a fortune teller, you can still interview your friends and family and find out how they feel about the product. Do you see a future in it?

Life Cycle of a Product or Business

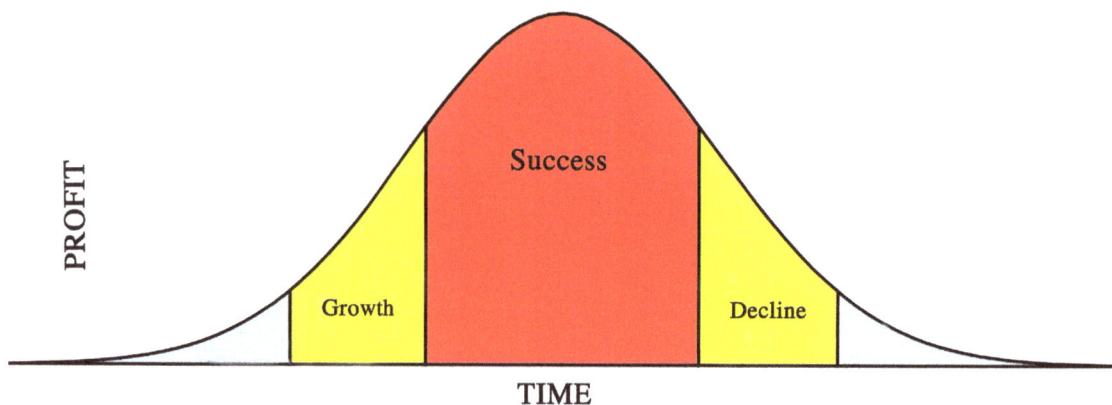

Teach me.

Is training included in the franchise fee? How many people can you train? How long is the training? What do you learn? What schedules and functions will you perform? Where must you travel to do the training? Are expenses additional? Do you have to pass a test? What happens if the franchisor doesn't approve of one of your employees? What kind of impression will your employee have after doing training with the franchisor? How much time will you spend training? Will you have to do more training later?

Normally, when you first open your franchise you will send a certain number of people to training or have them trained in your location. It's usually built into the startup costs. However, your general manager may leave or be a wash out within six months. Do you have to send your employees to San Diego for training when you're located in Chicago? There are hotel costs, airplane tickets and expenses. Will you now have to pay for the new training too?

Will the franchisor allow you to train all new employees in your location after you have been open a certain amount of time? How long will it be before they trust that you know what you are doing and that you can handle the training of new employees yourself?

The franchisor's training program should prepare you for operating and owning your own business. Several things create success: the length of the training program, assumptions as to the starting point of your skills, the instructors, real life situations, the training environment, the tests you must take to show you understand what they are teaching you, requirements: i.e. wearing a uniform, getting up at 4am to work a shift, handling money, etc. Can you operate the business on a daily basis? Can you perform management and staff functions? Can you handle the accounting, the decision-making process, inventory control, marketing, banking, cash flow, human resources, etc.?

My experience was that the franchisor was much more respectful of owners in training rather than the owner's employees. They wanted the training to be "real world" experiences so they really worked the managers and assistant managers hard, however, owners at times needed to be dealt with using kid gloves, and that's what they did. Some owners didn't want to wear hats, some complained that they wanted New York style bagels as a product; others didn't like to take tests. The franchisor handled all of them carefully, as though they would break. But the managers that came back had stories of being "worked to death" and not all of them were happy with their treatment.

⚜ ⚜ ⚜

Let me tell you more...

The franchisor made sure that each owner was trained for 3-6 weeks at the franchisor's corporate stores or at a franchise location nearby. The difference among standards was readily apparent when a group of us were sent to an individual owner's franchise location for day to work several different staff positions. We spent two hours or so working on food preparation, as a cashier, counting out cash drawers, etc. We were expected to eat there too, as the day was packed with activity and time was at a premium. At this particular location we watched the restaurant's own staff as they overloaded the food containers that were placed in the refrigerated moveable coolers (the lid stayed open to access the food), left food out too long and violated other health codes. The trainer from the corporation suggested we all stick with peanut butter sandwiches and had to report the violations back to headquarters.

⚜ ⚜ ⚜

Product tests.
Any franchise has to protect itself from getting "old" and feeling worn out to customers. With all the competition that abounds in the world now, every company must constantly refresh their products and find ways to intrigue new customers as well as keeping regular customers from getting bored. Especially in the restaurant arena, new product offerings are necessary to keep the menu and the restaurant "fresh" and trendy and to pull people in who have fallen by the wayside.

Does the franchisor have a means of determining what direction the market is going? Do they listen for feedback from the franchisees? Do they analyze data? Do they use outside industry consultants? Do they subscribe to a research sharing service? How accurate are they when they create a new product to capitalize on a trend? Does the franchisor supply sufficient information, trends, market costs, predictions, etc?

Some new products are offered for a limited time because they are seasonal or because they have a higher food cost. Some products are so popular that they are added to the regular menu.

How does the company test its products? Does it do focus groups? Does it continually test and develop new products to keep its products fresh? Where are its test markets (which major cities, what are the demographics, how long is the test)? Does the franchisor accurately know the product cost and the impact on franchisees of marketing a new product? Will the raw materials be available and at what cost? Does it tie into general market trends? How successful will it be? How will it be advertised?

Most franchisors will test market a new product before rolling it out to the general public. Sometimes, they choose a few "special" franchisees to do this. Many franchisors test new products with the most successful franchisees to enable success, to make sure the product is sold correctly, to give "status" to a franchisee, and to make sure test data is returned promptly. However, testing only with the most successful franchisees means that those franchisees that struggle may have problems introducing a new product. You have to figure that they are going to give it to the ones they know can do it right, so even if the chosen few experience successful sales, that doesn't necessarily mean that your crew of high-schoolers can accomplish the same thing. Each location has its own uniqueness due to the city, the owner, the employees, culture, etc. So what happens if the franchisee is forced to sell a product that "bombs" in his/her market? It can mean loss in having to carry inventory that won't be sold. It can mean negative feedback from customers because of their perception of an inferior product.

Will the franchisor "auto" ship a certain amount of product to you whether you want that much product or not? Can you change it if you want to be more conservative? Will you be out the cost of goods if you can't sell the product in your market?

When I signed my franchise agreement, the franchisor employed a vice president that was formerly from a prestigious business renowned for their food. The VP, also a chef, took great care in researching new food products and trends and was very creative. He left the company within a few years and the quality of the new products never seemed to have the same creativity with any of his replacements.

Franchisees are the greatest source of ideas. In my experience, the franchisor rarely wanted to acknowledge them. Although the franchise constantly asked for new ideas from the franchisees and even solicited them with forms for new product creations, I don't know of one idea that was actually tested or used.

⚜ ⚜ ⚜

Let me tell you more...

When franchisors bring out a new product or offers a limited time product for promotional purposes, they will often try to "sell" it to the franchisees. When we received the information showing what the end product would be, the ingredients and directions to make it, we would usually check the pricing they showed and see if the food costs per product were computed correctly. Most often, the costs were *incorrect* because a marketing department had created the materials and not an operational person.

Many of the franchisees called it an honor to be one of the test sites for new products that the franchisor developed. It was a way for us to have a voice about what products were successful and rolled out for everyone to sell. Usually, only the more successful and cooperative franchisees were asked to be a test market. I found that after the honor lost its bloom, I often ended up being left with high food costs and unprofitable products. We also had disgruntled customers that liked the product offering and then we had to tell them it was a test that failed and would no longer be available. Some of the test products were great in other areas of the country but not in ours, so we absorbed lost revenue because of waste.

If a franchisor maintains their own corporate stores and test products there first, they may have an entirely different cost ratio and not be able to accurately prove to you that a new product will work for you too. Since they supply their own products, they may be right down the street from the distribution center or manufacturing plant. They may not have the same delivery costs. The company may also discount the product to themselves so it's really tough to know if they can truly tell you that a new product is good for you financially without testing it among franchisees.

⚜ ⚜ ⚜

Clear, concise information.

Franchisors need to communicate several things to franchisees: reporting needs, achievements of other franchisees, problem resolutions, market trends, information on competitors, links to other franchisees, R & D plans, economic outlet for the franchise, etc. What is their method of communication? Do they have emails, newsletters, a chain of communication that comes through your business consultant? How do you learn about new things, success and issues?

Your architect or theirs.

If your franchise requires a physical location or building, the franchisor will most likely specify an architect or a few approved architects, a builder, or several from which to choose from, which will be involved in "building out" the location. This means that they finish the interior space to the franchisor's specifications, which could include dropped ceilings, flooring, cabinetry, seating, cooking stations, etc

Often, the architect and builder are from another state and you will be required to pay their expenses for travel. You will pay these contractors but they will be enforcing what the *franchisor* wants and you may have limited say about what goes on.

Your build out will also have to adhere to all state and local health or safety requirements and have to go through the permitting department. Sometimes, you may have to wait weeks for your plans to be reviewed and if changes are required, you have to go through the whole process again. That is where a really good architect and builder can help you if they foresee a problem and change the blueprints before you begin.

⚜ ⚜ ⚜

Let me tell you more...

If you have to build a new building or finish out a space in a leased building, most franchisors have approved builders, architects and contractors they want you to use. Just because you have the list, don't neglect to do your own research about them. One builder that was on my approved list, took a down payment from a new franchisee and immediately left town. Although the man had done satisfactory business with the franchisor for a few years, he was getting a divorce and wanted to skip town to get away from his wife and so he embezzled all the money. It was a nasty situation for the new franchisee as well as the franchisor who recommended him.

Other recommendations just might not work for you based on personality issues. I found it more to my benefit to hire my own architect, although the professional I chose had also worked for other franchisees in the chain. I also hired my own construction crew, one that was familiar with franchise requirements. That way I didn't have to pay an increased cost for the crew to come in from another city. One of the recommended contractors on the franchisor's list was two thousand miles away.

The inspection.

Franchisors need to perform inspections to make sure that a certain standard is being met. Inspections are often unannounced in order to be more accurate and for the franchisor to truly see how your operation is running. They can often include cleanliness, customer service as well as being timed for customer interaction, whether promotional materials are available and displayed, how busy the franchise is, how many customers are coming and going, adherence to policies, etc. My experience has been that a business consultant may walk in the door with an eighteen-page inspection questionnaire. The level of detail may seem extremely nitpicky. The representative from the corporation that reviews the franchise may or may not have certain "hot buttons" that he/she looks for and some can be aggravating to the franchisee. If the franchisee has managed to upset the franchisor in any way, an inspection that is so frustratingly detailed can be the result. Also, check to see what the contract allows if the franchisor finds things in violation of their policies. Can they shut you down? How long do you have to rectify the situation? Can they make you purchase additional equipment?

Who's behind the scenes?

The staff and support staff of a franchisor is the franchisee's lifeblood. Make sure you meet their business and marketing support staff. Do they have people assigned to territories? How many franchisees does a consultant share, how often are they in the field? Do they return their phone calls within twenty-four hours and is it a company policy? How many different people will you have to contact for issues with equipment, training, policies, shipments, product, marketing, etc. How long has the support staff been in the industry and how are they trained? How much authority do they have or do they constantly have to go back to headquarters to get permission to allow you to digress from the norm or help you solve your problems?

Let me tell you more....

The business consultants that arrived in our store to assist with our opening stayed about two weeks and one was fairly new in his job and the other was an extremely knowledgeable and dedicated person. The newer consultant had a quirky personality, which rubbed many of my employees the wrong way and at one point made a cashier cry. The other consultant was so enthusiastic about his job that he called for long meetings after every day where all the managers had to rehash what went right and what went wrong. Great idea, however, when everyone was at the point of exhaustion I had to step in and let him know we were too tired to give or hear any more feedback. He wasn't pleased about it but did back off. I wasn't sure if he would report back to the franchisor that we were uncooperative, however, we ended up getting an award from the franchisor for the best grand opening.

Corporate culture.

One of the things that a franchise brings to you is their corporate culture. Is it formal or casual, friendly or reserved, profit driven or grassroots creative? You have to make sure that you really mesh with who the people are that will provide your support, marketing and new products. You need to tour the franchisor's building and see how the employees work. Is there a level of excitement or a feeling of drudgery? Those employees are also working for you and you must make sure you feel comfortable interfacing with them and feel secure in what they can do for you. What is their education level? How do they treat minorities and women, is there anything that they believe or do that would jeopardize your success? Are there cultural differences? Do they share information? Do they have fun? Do they wear suits or casual clothes? All those things affect you as you bind yourself to them. What is their experience in doing business in the U.S. and internationally? What is their background in business?

So after you see the franchisor's culture, you have to decide what type of company culture you will have for your own site, how both can blend together and how you want your employees and your customers to feel. How will you communicate? Will you allow any employee to talk to any manager or just the one that they are assigned to report to? Will you provide incentive programs to generate excitement? Will you expect an employee to do their job without providing positive feedback? Will it be profit driven only or will you want to accomplish something else such as being a force in your community?

How will you motivate employees to give their best? Will you have fun, play games, issue monetary bonuses, name a "most valuable player?" As an owner, you have to be the one to decide on the tone of your business and then make sure that all the employees buy into it and that your customers feel comfortable with it.

Let's all get along.

What if the franchisor doesn't seem to like you after you've been in business for a while? Logically, if you are giving them money it shouldn't matter, but what if the franchisor has a friend that wants your territory? What if they have others just waiting to take your spot that will buy even more territories? Anything you do can be perceived negatively if you operate outside of their contract. Not everything is etched in stone. Many times, there are just conflicts of personalities or different interpretations of policies. What if the corporation says you have to be open on Sundays and you are in a downtown area with absolutely no customers? Make sure you get an agreement *upfront* that is legally binding and allows you to stay closed on Sundays.

What if the company discontinues a product but your regional area demands you still carry it and since it is easy to do, you decide to continue offering it? Will the franchisor penalize you? Will they see you as a renegade?

Most franchisees are unique people and perhaps they want to wear a cowboy heat when meeting their customers but the franchisor expects you to wear a baseball cap with their logo. What type of punishment do you incur? The cold shoulder or an out and out war?

Respond with direct questions, ask for documentation as to what the franchisor is unhappy with, ask for an action plan to correct items, discuss this with your business consultant and then proceed up the ladder of authority until you get a good explanation. Seek legal advice if you feel targeted. Talk to the franchise association.

Let me tell you more...

Going to conventions hosted by the franchisor allowed me to see who was in the good graces of the owners. The owners, their Chief Financial Officer, the corporate lawyer on staff and other executives hosted dinner tables and breakfast tables and only those franchisees that were friendly with the owners, in the good graces of the owners and were high achieving locations were invited to sit there. The rest of the franchisees sat among themselves. One franchisee was consistently invited to those tables. He had the highest grossing locations in sales by far, having exceeded the sales by several million dollars from the rest of the franchisees due to his special location and being able to be open twenty-four hours a day. This particular franchisee seemed to be on extremely friendly terms with the owners. After a few years, the franchisee (whom I will call "L.S.") opened a new business that had one or two similarities with the existing businesses but were largely very different too.

The franchisors of the existing businesses were very upset that L.S. opened these new businesses and sued L.S. for violation of the non-compete clause that was incorporated into the franchise agreement. They demanded the surrender of the locations to the corporation. As heard through the grapevine of franchisees, L.S.'s lawyer told him to surrender the locations and then countersue, which he did. The lawsuit dragged on for a couple of years. The court said that the non-compete clause was unenforceable and found in favor of L.S. A franchise association from another type of business then got involved, trying to uphold the franchisor's position that the non-compete clause was valid (the association was trying to make sure that this court case did not set a precedent) but was knocked down. The settlement figure is not available information but was rumored to be in the millions.

This situation centered not only on a franchisee opening another business that may or may not compete with the existing businesses, but because this was the most successful franchisee in the chain, the other remaining franchisees became alarmed that they might be taken over if they proved to be very successful, and thus their location could be turned into a corporate store, making all the money for the franchisor.

Distribution is different than manufacturing.

Franchisors negotiate contracts with suppliers. The more they buy, the cheaper the price but the goods still have to be distributed to the franchisees which also adds to the cost of the product. If a franchisor is big enough, they will have their own distribution network. That means that all raw materials, products, etc. that have to be delivered to your franchise door will be delivered directly by the franchisor. This means greater control over time of delivery, costs, product and quality. However, having a distribution division is costly and most smaller franchisors cannot afford this and will have to subcontract the delivery. This means that you are not only at the mercy of the franchisor to negotiate good terms with the distributor, but also at the distributor's mercy when it comes to your delivery time and window. You may have to unload the truck yourself which means having to pay for extra labor to do so. You may have to allow them access to your building after hours and accept a "drop". How much leeway will distributors have in getting the product to your location, time of day, days of the week, etc.? How many employees need to help unload? If the schedule is not etched in stone, how much will having an employee stand by add to your labor cost?

Some franchisors insist that you take delivery during the night when no one is there. That means that you must give the delivery driver access to the building and hope he remembers to set the alarm again before he leaves. The distributor just "drops" the product without it being checked for accuracy. Do you trust someone in your building at night alone? Do you have anything else that you may jeopardize by allowing this? Many franchises never have an issue with this, but if you have a driver that is transient and just doesn't have the work ethic you expect, you can likely anticipate some issues occurring.

You need to know what back up options exist for a truck that breaks down, if your order is mixed up, or if the truck delivers someone else's order. It does happen.

A franchisor may manufacture their own products such as tortilla chips. They still have to make it to your location through a distribution network. They may own their own distribution network and have trucks that deliver products to your site. If the franchisor determines that the cost is no longer feasible and needs to sub-contract the deliveries, you will likely have little say so in whom they choose. They may choose someone located across the country that doesn't often make deliveries to your location. The new distributor may not respond to you as they would to a larger client.

Food costs are a big issue in a restaurant. Although a new distributor may guarantee lower food costs, what about surcharges for higher gas and oil prices? What about shortages? Who gets priority?

⚜ ⚜ ⚜

Let me tell you more...

My franchisor originally owned their own distribution company too, and owned trucks with lift gates. It was really easy for the truck driver to pull a pallet to the back, operate the lift gate and the product was delivered. This only required one driver on the truck. The distribution was wonderful and the company was customer service driven. I was very comfortable with all the drivers and always made sure they had a cold drink or food if they were hungry. Unfortunately, the lift gates needed constant repairs and the cost to run the distribution company was too much for the franchisor.

The franchisor sold off their trucks, found a third party distribution company and signed a contract to have them distribute all their products. Instead of the company being located where the franchisor was headquartered, the new distributor was located farther away from the largest group of core franchisees. Although the initial contract spelled out just how much they could sell the product to all the franchisees, it also allowed for fuel surcharges and that meant that each delivery cost up to $100 more because it was farther away. We took two deliveries a week so we ended up paying over $10,000 more per year for our products.

Although the distributor had promised the franchisor that over a period of time, the cost per case of product to deliver would come down, it did not. The franchisor was not large enough to put any strength behind their arguments and the franchisees absorbed the brunt of the problems in rising product costs. We also had no input and no clout.

After many missed products on our deliveries, which included all franchise locations, the distributor agreed that if it were their fault, they would overnight the product to us. We missed many cases of ham on one shipment and when we received their overnight delivery through a shipping company, we opened the cases to find the product already at 80 degrees (far beyond food safe temperatures) and the meat had been packed with only two cold packs, the kind you would put in a lunchbox.

⚜ ⚜ ⚜

Product specifications.

Some franchisors will insist that everything be purchased through them. Sometimes bad, sometimes good. What if a supplier goes out of business; what if a supplier splits with the franchisor; what if the product deteriorates? Generic products *or* those products that you don't use in case type quantities should be allowed to be purchased through wholesale clubs, or local food distributors who can do a better or cheaper job. Being able to get competitive quotes can not only help your cost but also allows you a "fallback" position to get a product if the franchisor's truck is stuck in the snow.

The franchisor sets the specifications for all products. They usually have a formula they believe will make you successful. For example, if you are a restaurant and their target food cost is 30%, then you need to make sure that you do not have any extra waste so you can make the target. You may have higher fixed costs than other franchisees if you have a premium location. The standard profit margin may drive you out of business so it may be extremely important that you are allowed to find your own source of supply on some items.

⚜ ⚜ ⚜

Let me tell you more...

The franchisor subcontracted with a very large, well known firm to make the franchisor's recipes for soups, vacuum pack and freeze them. We would get them in our shipments and they would be dropped into simmering water and heated until they were at the correct temperature. The franchisor had no control over the conditions in the manufacturing facility, although I'm sure their contract must have stated terms for cleanliness and handling.

One of the other franchisees had a customer find a metal bolt in their soup one day. Luckily, the customer didn't swallow it or break any teeth, but it goes to show you that you don't have control over everything. There is also no way to prove that the soup came in with the bolt in it and that the franchisee did not accidentally expose the customer to the bolt. In situations like that, the franchisee would write a report to the franchisor, the franchisor would contact the manufacturer and they would start an investigation. By the time all that happened, a problem was never found. It is a lesson that many things are outside your control when you buy a franchise.

⚜ ⚜ ⚜

Full disclosure.

Many franchisors will insist that they be given access to your profit and loss information or Point of Sale information daily. This is designed to keep you honest, however, is it really any of their business what you make or spend as long as you pay your royalties? Many feel this a violation of privacy but you are not likely to get around this policy. With the ease of the Internet and nightly polling of your computer, you will likely have to adhere to this.

Most franchisors will poll your computer during night (data from your computer is transmitted via Internet lines back to the franchisor) to determine what you made in sales that day, any other reports they want and just how much you owe them in royalties. Most require a percentage of sales for royalties. In today's digital world, most will require an automatic bank draft from your bank account with what you owe them. That can put you in a cash flow problem if you need to pay a large invoice.

Remodeling.

What if five years after you've signed on to a franchise and been in business the franchise decides to remodel its décor, can they force you to remodel your store, too? This can be a substantial cost and not only put you out of business, but be a means by which the franchisor could take over your franchise and drive you into bankruptcy. Make sure that any changes that are to be allowed are spelled out as to when, what, where, and how much. In your agreement, it needs to be as specific as possible, not just say that every five years, cosmetic changes will be required? Does replacing composite counters with granite counters, installing custom designed cabinetry or reupholstering customer seating for 200 fall under cosmetic? Do you define cosmetic as paint color, flooring and upholstery?

⚜ ⚜ ⚜

Let me tell you more...

Every franchise needs to stay current with the trends of their particular industry. In the restaurant business, décor is one thing that needs to stay current if not on the cutting edge. However, the décor is NOT the *main* reason why a person chooses to dine in a particular establishment. The franchisor will often integrate remodeling into their contract terms. How often the décor is changed and the design could very well be the difference between the franchisee ever making a profit or not. You should expect that the frequency of remodeling and the cost be spelled out in the contract.

My experience was that the franchisor decided at one point that a very new, more contemporary design should be implemented and announced that all restaurants with a design that was five years old must remodel their location to the new design as well as any new locations being built. The company hired a restaurant designer and together they created a very different look for the locations. It included the most expensive textiles, woods and granite to make the restaurants look upscale. After a preliminary check of the cost to reproduce the design, it was scaled back as the cost ended up being as much to build a new location. Most business loans are ten-year loans so trying to even *get* another loan after just five years could be impossible. So add the cost of your current loan payment to another loan payment for nearly the same amount and you have no profit and are losing money.

Going back to the drawing board, the design was scaled back and went through many permutations. The owners did not allow suggestions from the current franchisees because of an attitude that the franchisor knew better than the franchisees doing business daily. Two of us were caught in the middle of building a new location and were instructed to go with the new design. Commercial carpet squares were specified in a magenta and tan color, a water fountain with boulders was specified, as well as walls around booths to give the dining room a more cozy feel. Also, to add to the coziness, glass panels were to be installed on the walls above the booths. The initial design was very attractive, however, again the cost was so prohibitive (over $50,000 in decorative glass panels alone) that it was redesigned so that the glass sat only in a bracket and was to be cut in a triangular shape with a point facing upwards (a sharp one.)

Trendier colors were specified for the walls with white woodwork throughout. Three thousand dollars worth of artwork done on Masonite boards (not even canvas) was to be installed. The bathrooms were to be done in "circus" colors. The kitchen area held no storage because there was no room, with all the space being allocated to the dining room to hold more seating. I was able to lobby for a different design for the bathrooms that was more neutral.

After paying an architect nearly $20,000 to incorporate the design into my new location, I was upset at some of the design elements. I asked the owner to allow the location to be built without the carpet. My argument was that the carpet (especially the light colors chosen) would show all stains and would be a maintenance issue in a busy restaurant. He initially said that the squares could be changed out if stained (at a cost of over $20 per square) but then told me I did not have to install them. I did not get it in writing and he later said he didn't remember telling me that so insisted they be put in, and they were, but at least in a smaller area.

The glass above the booths was installed with a point so sharp that they would have decapitated anyone falling on them. After seeing them, the franchisor's business consultant insisted they be removed. I had been told they were tempered glass by the restaurant designer but upon removal, we found them to be regular glass that broke into super sharp shards and would have impaled anyone unlucky enough to break them. If the owners would have insisted they stay, no insurance policy could have ever been enough to cover the havoc they would have caused.

The white woodwork lasted about two weeks before it had to be painted brown. Mopping and wear and tear caused it to stain immediately. The walls around the booths were a constant challenge to clean. In one area, the design was for the walls to be eight feet high for additional privacy. Because you could not see into this area from the counters, we nicknamed this area "the make out room" because no one could tell what was going on there. The liability you can incur if something happens in your restaurant is staggering. This became an area that had to be visited constantly by management and was also the area where parents let their children color on the walls and splash soup onto the sage green paint.

The water fountain was a series of rocks sitting on top of one another with no support or interlocking systems. This was removed, also after the business consultant told the owners it just wouldn't work.

After this very frustrating experience, the restaurant designer was fired and the architect was brought on to create an even newer design and I was left with a restaurant that didn't fit in to either the old or the new layout. The cost of this design was approximately $380,000 for just the build out alone.

⚜ ⚜ ⚜

Get it in writing.

When you sign a contract, obviously not every situation can be covered in just one document. However, each and every situation that you can think of that may be an issue should be spelled out in as much detail as possible. A verbal agreement will not cut it five years later when the franchisor cannot recall the conversation.

⚜ ⚜ ⚜

Let me tell you more....

As mentioned in the example above, after having a location for two years, I prepared for opening the second location. The specifications in the restaurant design had changed and the franchisor wanted to use my new location to showcase the changes. One change was the installation of carpet, which I felt would not be good. I could not see the advantage of having to use a carpet cleaner constantly after observing that the interior designer had specified a color of carpet that would show every bit of food ground into the carpet. I objected heavily to this new requirement and the V.P. told me verbally that I would not have to do it.

When we came to installing the flooring, which was a few months later, he changed his mind and actually told me he had forgotten ever talking to me about the subject. Since by that time other franchisees were getting their blueprints done and they incorporated the new changes, the V.P. said he could not take any heat from other franchisees about the same issue so I would have to install carpet. We finally compromised and allowed the carpet to be installed in a small cozy sitting area and not the entire dining room. It was my naïveté to accept something verbally and I should have asked that he initially send the permission not to use carpet in an email. I could also have sent him and email confirming our conversation so I would have had a record of it.

⚜ ⚜ ⚜

The uber wealthy.

Do the franchisors live in an ivory tower now or do they get their hands dirty? If they have lost touch with the franchise owner and what he/she needs to serve his/her customers, it can have far reaching effects. Although many franchisors start out running a small business themselves and then progress to owning a larger company and selling franchises, how well do they remember the grind and the pressures? They may have a totally different lifestyle now if they are successful and enjoy driving that Maserati. Will you be able to communicate your complaints or needs?

Bad decisions at the top affect all franchises. I have no doubt that the franchisors had exquisite taste in some things. They dressed immaculately, drove beautiful, expensive cars and had their offices decorated luxuriously. However, when it came time to choose between what was really important in a new product, new packaging or choosing a new manufacturing partner, I wasn't always convinced they had the franchisees best interests in mind.

An Extra Helping of Caution - Getting Fired by a Franchisor

No one wants to think about it but generally the franchise agreement is geared to protect the franchisor, not the franchisee. You may be so excited to start your business and you may feel that you will be the exception to the rule and that the "rules" are only there to weed out the bad few.

You just can't predict what will happen in the coming years to the people who own the company, the weather, the other franchisees, the product, society or new laws passed that may affect your business. You need to make sure YOU are protected too and have written reassurance that promises made to you will be kept. Many franchisees receive a handshake on certain deals only to find that it has no meaning once they open for business.

Recently, California attempted to enact new legislation that affects franchises called The Fair Franchise Act. It did not get passed into law. It is based on a recent situation where McDonald's fired a franchisee who had been with them for thirty years. (Most franchise contracts last for a term of ten years and then must be renewed for another ten years.) The franchisee had no recourse since the franchise agreement was at the end of its current term. The franchisee was able to sell off the equipment but nothing else. Originally, McDonald's was going to allow them to sell the franchise to someone new because McDonald's said they would continue the lease, but then changed their mind. The franchisee lost their livelihood and any investment they had not recouped. The agreement was written to protect the franchisor and thus, the franchisee was at the end of their association. No reason was cited by McDonald's as to why they fired this franchisee.

⚜ ⚜ ⚜

Let me tell you more…

Sometimes another franchisee will do something that affects everyone else. For example, one franchisee thought that since he owned one franchise location he could open another under an entirely *different* name and still use the products but bypass the royalties he should be paying. He wrongly assumed that since the new location was named something different, no one would ever discover the similarities in the products. He was incorrect on so many levels including that since many of the products were supplied by the current franchisor, they would be able to put two and two together and realize that his location was ordering a lot more product but not showing an increase in sales. No one could spend all that extra money without showing a return. Also, people in the community were bound to talk, write reviews, etc. thus helping spread the word about a new place with surprising similarities to the current franchise.

The franchisor sent a business consultant from another territory to dine at the new place and look around. He was seasoned enough to know immediately what was going on so he documented and took pictures of everything. The franchisor sued them, had them shut down and took back the original franchise. They made a deal with the building's owner and leased the store, gave a minimal amount to the franchisee for the equipment and then sold it all to a new owner at a substantial profit.

Afterwards, because of the actions of one franchisee, it soured the business for all the rest of the franchises since the franchisor was now on their guard warning everyone not to try the same thing. Instead of interacting in a positive way, communication now became negative. In this case, the franchisor was wronged and the actions of one franchisee seemed to change the way they looked at the rest of us.

⚜ ⚜ ⚜

How badly do they want you?

Contracts with the franchisor are really the basis of your relationship. Make sure to have an attorney review them and go over them with a fine tooth comb. Some franchisors will negotiate points if they want you bad enough.

The contract will cover points such as your territory, royalties, franchise fees, term of contract, renewal fees, conditions for refunds, payment systems, other money you may be expected to spend on such things as grand openings, standards you must maintain, confidentiality, terms of construction, locations and approvals required for contractors, advertising and promotional responsibilities, operational responsibilities, conditions of resale, inspections, terminations of contract clauses, and schedules of openings, etc.

Very importantly, the contract will include waivers of liability for the *franchisor* for any hot water the *franchisee* gets himself into with the landlord, utility companies, the government, etc. Don't think that if you have a problem, the franchisor will stand by you or even offer you advice when it comes to legal issues. They will want to maintain a distance from you so that they are not implicated in any poor decisions you make if it might jeopardize them.

The contract.

Many franchisors will have certain requirements as to the agreement you sign with the landlord, i.e. the lease. The franchisor will most likely include build out requirements as to the amount of electricity, water, sewer, air conditioning and other utilities required. They will show that they are NOT required to pay the lease in case the franchisee defaults but they will likely include a clause that says they have the right to take over the lease. They will require a certain amount of parking.

The lease will also specify exactly what you are responsible for. Even though the landlord owns the building and must maintain the grounds, the franchisee may be responsible for any broken windows. You may be responsible for cleaning your sidewalk or maintaining the area around the dumpster. Make sure every item is as specific as possible to prevent disputes later.

Most franchises that have a building and location that you must rent or own, require a certain décor to make sure that locations across the country are standard. Décor usually stays trendy for 5- 10 years, depending on the designer, the materials used, the colors on the walls, etc. Some flooring may be worn out in high traffic areas; some tile or wall colors will have outlived their trendiness.

The franchisor may require you to remodel or update the look of the business to continue to attract customers. This is especially true in the restaurant business. Will it be cosmetic or will it include moving walls and cabinets. Some fast food franchises actually require that the entire building be torn down and rebuilt every ten or twenty years. You must make a lot of profit to be able to afford a new building. Ten years ago, most places were using Formica counters and now the standard is granite which is a much more expensive material. Having to remodel a location can cost almost as much to build a location from scratch. You need to make sure the guidelines for requirements are spelled out in the contract. Will they cap the expense you must make at $100,000 or not? Will they require a remodel in five years or ten? Who gets to say what specifications there are? A professional? A consortium of franchise owners? The franchisor with no input from the franchisees? Get it spelled out upfront!

How long does it last?

Usually a franchise fee covers the right to be a franchise for a specified length of time, most often for ten years. If you are doing well, and want to carry on your agreement, you may have to pay additional fees to renew your contract. This is where the franchisor can "get" you. If you already have the experience, the location and most likely the building, will you want to change tracks and go into a different line of business? Probably not. However, a renewal fee of $30,000 could really eat into your profits that first year after renewal.

Since the length of the contract is most likely ten years, it coincides with many business loans, as they must be paid back within ten years. So, at the end of the contract term, you would have paid back your initial business loan and your franchise contract would expire. This leaves you an out. However, to renew your franchise rights, there may be a renewal fee, which could be substantial. You need to know this upfront. If you must remodel, pay a hefty fee, or add equipment, then you will be talking to the bank again to try and get another loan. Just when you thought you would be making greater profit, you could become saddled with more debt.

You are really like the franchisor's employee.

The philosophy of the franchisor is similar to that of a CEO that runs his own company. Although a franchisee is not technically an employee of the franchise and the franchisee should be making money for the franchisor, the decisions of the owner impacts the franchisees in every way. Does the owner believe in the best and most luxurious décor or is it bargain basement? Does the owner have good taste, is he well educated, is he multi- culturally educated, where and how does he live? Although this is a business arrangement, you will be tied to this person's company for years. You must respect each other, be able to work together and believe in the company's decision-making abilities and processes.

They may want to be in industry leader and be known for innovative products. Or, they may want to just be "me too" in an industry and follow the leader and imitate them instead of doing a lot of research and development. The franchisor may make choices that benefits them as a company, such as narrowing protected territories to perhaps only a mile away so other franchises may be sold very close to you. *Caution - your contract may often give the franchisor the right to change policies without your consent.*

Reports and more reports.

Most franchise systems have a Point of Sale (POS) system that you use to record all of your transactions and sales. It is basically an electronic cash register that is tied into a back office computer and accumulates information about your sales. We are also beginning to see new systems with of the use of iPads and Smartphones as sales devices. The newer systems are also used to send email receipts, customer loyalty emails and be more portable than traditional systems. Sales can be broken down by hour, category of product, weekly, monthly, etc. giving you fingertip access to almost any information that you need. This gives you a more defined control of what goes on in your business.

At the cash register, assume you sold a product, received the money from a customer and the POS system recorded the sale, and told you what change to give to the customer. At the same time, the POS system accumulated the items sold, provided you with marketing reports showing you how much of any one item you sold, the most popular items, and may interfaced with your inventory system to show you how many of any one item you have left in stock.

This is great information for you to have and the franchisor may also want your information. The franchisor also wants to see your sales to know how much to expect in royalties. Based on your contract, you may have no way to prevent their intrusion into your system, and no way to protect your privacy.

The franchisor will specify what type of reporting you must do. They will, of course, want to see your sales so that they will know what royalties you owe them. Most of the point of sale systems (POS) make this rather foolproof so that if you ring up a sale it will automatically merge with the royalty reports. They will specify a due date so that if you complete a week of sales, they may require that you send a royalty report to them the following day and make the royalty payment within seven days. They may also want to see your profit and loss reports. This is a sticky issue because this is your confidential information. The franchisor may desire this information to keep track of the average profit margin to enable them to sell more franchises accurately or to enable them to stave off problems with costs.

In my experience, unless the franchisor has created their own formulas and specified in very narrow terms exactly what goes into each line item on a P & L, then the information is not entirely accurate. For example, a franchisor may write off his personal cell phone because he makes some calls for the business. Technically, if he uses it for his own personal use, then not all of the cell phone costs should be written off. Some accountants are looser than others when advising their clients as to what to include for allowable expenses.

Profit and loss reports can really only be compared when everything else is equal. Wages vary across the country, cost per square foot of lease space varies, management skills vary, as well as the skill level and expertise of the owner.

Most franchisors will specify the software you must use to submit reports for sales, profitability, labor, etc. You may be required to purchase proprietary software (developed by the franchisor) and certain computer hardware. If so, then what happens when it becomes outdated? Must you still purchase from the franchisor or can you shop around on the open market?

Sample Profit and Loss Statement

Revenue After Taxes

Sales (without sales tax)	1,695,000

Cost of Goods Sold

Food	499,050
Packaging	55,300
Labor	601,780
Total Cost of Goods Sold	**1,156,130**

Gross Profit on Sale	**538,870**

Operating Expenses

Utilities	36,000
Repairs and Maintenance	1400
Cash Shortage	360
Cleaning	21,600
Phone/Internet	5,400
Office Supplies	2,200
Printing	3,300
Kitchen Supplies	2,550
Uniforms	3,300
Grand Opening Expenses	9,000
Total Controllable Expenses	**85,110**

Profit After Controllables	**453,760**

Non-Controllable Expenses

Royalties	84,750
Advertising Royalties	33,900
Rent, Common Area Maintenance	136,776
Local Advertising	6,000
Security Monitoring	240
Accountant, Legal	1,300
Bank Charges	420
Credit Card Service Fees	14,700
Pest Control	1,440
Bed Debt	0
Insurance	14,400
Satellite Music	1,332
Licenses, Permits	600
Taxes	4,992
Deprecitation	5,400
Loan Payments	63,000
Total Non Controllables	**369,250**

Net Income	**84,510**
Add Back Depreciation	**5,400**
Net Cash Flow	**89,910**

Financial Detail Report

Page 1 of 2	Print Date	: 6/12	
Store	Report Period	: 5/30	To 6/11

All Revenue Centers **Current Open Sales Day** : Monday, June 12

Net Sales $30,997.49		Beginning GC Total $4,079.02	Change In GC Total $32,560.01		Grand Control Total $36,639.03
Transaction Count	3,689	Checks Opened	3,471	** Eat In **	$20,309.96
Sales Per Transaction	$8.40	Checks Closed	3,471	++ Take Out ++	$8,733.66
Items Sold	22,524	Current Open Checks	0	## Phone ##	$1,953.87
Items Per Transaction	6.11	Sales Per Open Check	$8.93	Net Sales	$30,997.49
Void + Zero Transaction	188	Customer Count	3,471		
No Sale Count	266	Customers Per Check	1.00		
		Net Sales / Customer Count	$8.93	G Void/Ref/Ws	$153.44

Over / Short

Cash	$20,6??			
Checks	$0.0?			
Bank Deposit Cash	65)			
Short	.73)		**Short**	**($32.73)**

Sales

Department	Count	Sales	% Of Sales		
Bakery	3 ?	?,554.67	14.05%		
Beverage	2	?2.45	15.07%		
Breakfast	.	$?,047.52	3.23%		
Deli	15,?	$21,914.50	67.62%		
Miscellaneous		$7.43	0.02%		
Department Gross Sales	?,524	**$32,406.57**	100.00%	**Gross Sales**	**$32,406.57**

Media

	?unt	Amount	% Of Sales		
Open Item Disco	-1	$2.20	-0.01%		
Man?? r Discoun	86	($649.93)	2.10%		
?? e Meal D? ?nt	174	($593.05)	1.91%		
? Disc??	5	($33.31)	0.11%		
Dol?? ? V? ?cher	13	($37.07)	0.12%		
?wl S?	4	($13.96)	0.05%		
??? Half ?	4	($13.56)	0.04%		
Fr? ?	4	($6.06)	0.02%		
Free ??g Bev	6	($8.94)	0.03%		
Free Item	12	($43.40)	0.14%		
$1 OFF	12	($12.00)	0.04%		
All Discounts:		**($1,409.08)**	**4.55%**		**($1,409.08)**
				Net Sales:	**$30,997.49**
Sales Tax	3,250	$2,128.61	$30,394.65		
Taxes		**$2,128.61**			**$2,128.61**
				Net Sales + Tax	**$33,126.10**
Gift Certificate Sold	1	$10.00			
Receipts / Payments		**$10.00**			**$10.00**
				Balance	**$33,136.10**
Cash	4,780	$20,667.38			
Gift Card Redeem	3	$19.80			
Visa	674	$8,924.93			
Master Card	119	$1,689.63			
American Express	94	$1,422.81			
Discover	33	$411.55			
Payment Media Totals:		**$33,136.10**			**$33,136.10**

Location is everything.

A location can be judged on many things. A good location will have easy access to all directions without confusing driveways and signage. It should be visible to the road and not hidden by trees or blocked by other buildings. It may need to be in a "big box" shopping center to pull in more traffic. Make sure nothing is allowed to obstruct its view from the road.

Often, locations for franchises are in shopping centers. If this is the case, then what store is the draw for the center and pulls customers in? What happens if it goes out of business? What happens if the shopping center becomes only half occupied. These are all questions that need to be answered, as they impact your business and how you can protect yourself by including clauses in your lease. For example, you can include a reduced rent requirement if the occupation of the shopping center drops below 70%. You may be able to include an "opt out" clause if your sales are not as high as anticipated or you may be able to include a "rent as a percentage of sales" to protect you if the location does not pan out.

Many franchisors have a real estate consultant on staff who will help direct you to the better locations. You still need to make sure that they don't over estimate the value of the location because most likely they will be from out of state. It will be your money they want to spend if the location has a high per square footage cost.

Franchisors have a model or typical customer and they want your location to be located in the heart of them. They can tell you the average amount of money he/she makes, the number of times they visit your business on average, the type of neighborhood they live in, whether they are single, married or have children as well as a host of other things that make them the most likely to patronize your business. Using those attributes enables them to look at the demographics of locations to determine if your business would be a good fit or not.

There are many services that provide demographics including the number of cars that drive down a particular street. Market and demographics include the amount of traffic nearby, the number of households broken down by income, the amount of populations by age and race, education levels, whether people are married or have children, the amount of houses compared with apartments and all the logistics of what makes up a consumer.

CHOOSING A LOCATION

The best way to guarantee success

WHAT ARE THE DEMOGRPAHICS OF THE AREA?

Are your target customers close by? What's the population density? Do they have the disposable income to spend on your product? Is there lots of traffic driving by that will see your business? Is the location near households or businesses?

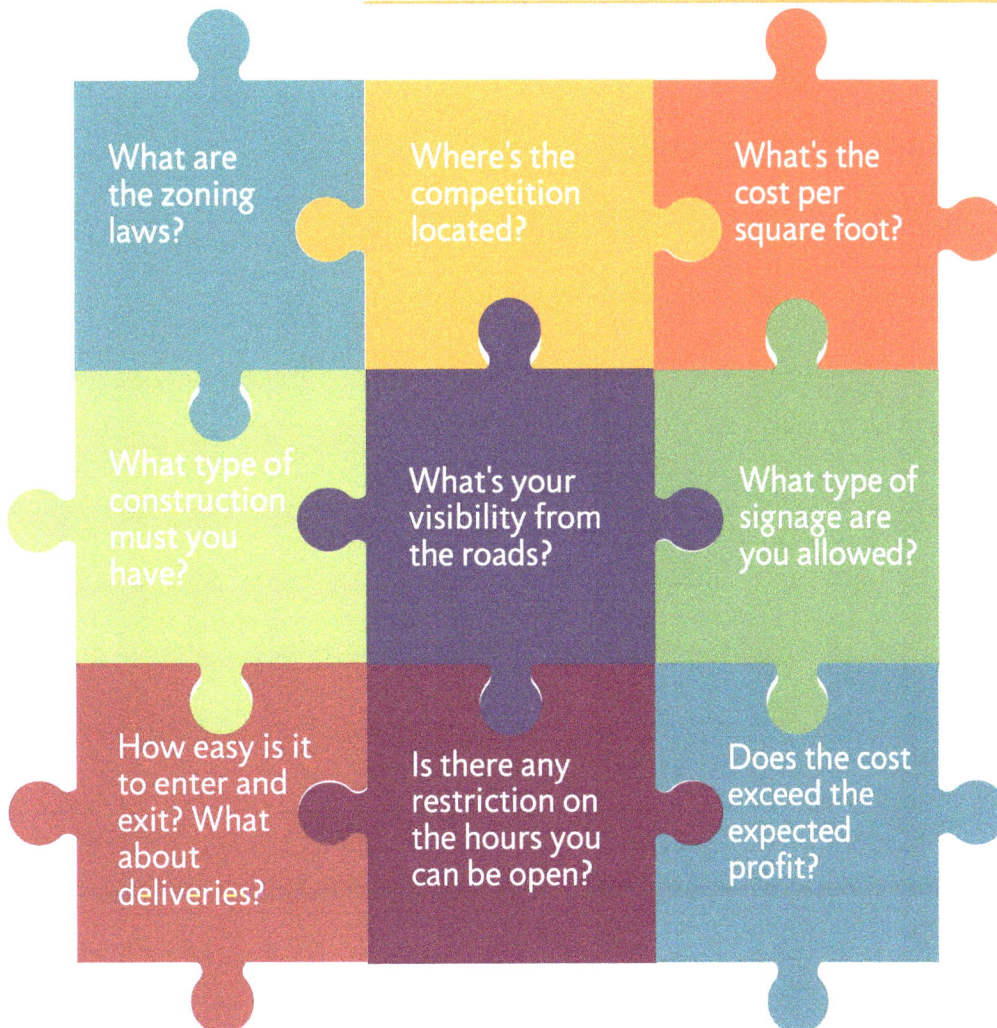

What are the zoning laws?

Where's the competition located?

What's the cost per square foot?

What type of construction must you have?

What's your visibility from the roads?

What type of signage are you allowed?

How easy is it to enter and exit? What about deliveries?

Is there any restriction on the hours you can be open?

Does the cost exceed the expected profit?

The landlord.

Not only will you be tied to the franchisor, you will also be associated with your landlord for a number of years. The landlord can affect your business in so many ways. Everything about the premises matters to your customers from pot holes in the parking lot to ease of access into the lot, from how hard the exterior doors are to open to how easy it is to exit the shopping center. Did the landlord plant bushes that attract bees right next to your front door? Do they clean the sidewalks weekly? Is there room for delivery trucks to park at your rear door or do they block cars? Do you have to clean your own windows? What about awnings? Do you pay their real estate taxes, their insurance, or other items that can fluctuate? How much allowance do you get off your rent for having to build out the space according to the franchisor? Do you have to pay their impact fees (fees paid to local government to pay for new roads, water lines, sewer, etc. usually based on the type of business you are)?

How much do they care about your presence? Do they feel you are important to their business mix or are you just a number? Will they listen to you if there is a leak in the ceiling and how fast will they get it repaired? Many people have landed in the landlord business because they had extra money to invest but really don't know the ins and outs of running a commercial property. Make sure your landlord is really experienced.

⚜ ⚜ ⚜

Let me tell you more…

Most cities and counties have what they call impact fees for any business. The justification for this is that certain businesses will require road construction, leave more waste to be processed, or impact the land in some way. It makes sense to charge the businesses, landlord or developer for this, however, some fees can increase drastically between the time a shopping center is zoned and the time it is actually built out. In many leases, the landlord will pass on these fees to the tenant. If you sign a lease without knowing the current fees, you may find that they can be exorbitant and set you back.

In one center, the fees had increased so much that it would have required an amendment to the financing for my restaurant to be able to afford them. The landlord of the shopping center, luckily, had enough pull with the county that he argued the fees should only be what he knew about when he received commercial zoning status and not what the county had changed them to. He was allowed to pay the lower of the two, however, not all landlords would have known to do that or have enough influence to pull it off.

In most leases if you have a building, you are responsible for all the windows and glass. It would make sense to me that because you are leasing the building that the landlord should be responsible, but that is not usually the case. The landlord is responsible for all the sidewalks, however, and their maintenance. In one building, I had lots of windows and the landlord, the actual owner of a large development company, lived nearby and had his offices nearby to my location. He used to cycle on Sunday mornings with a large group and they would stop at my restaurant for coffee and breakfast. There was no place to leave the groups' bicycles other than to lean them up against the walls or the windows. The landlord would always stop me to say that I needed to install bike racks for the group before one of them broke a window by shoving their bike against the glass. The irony of this was not lost on me, he was telling me that he was not willing to install the racks on *his* sidewalks but also letting me know that "something" could happen to the glass that I was responsible for.

Resale value.

Once you are running your franchise, you may want to sell your business for a multitude of reasons. You may have grown weary of ownership, have personal issues that prevent you from working as hard as needed, you may have made it a success so you feel it is the right time to sell to maximize your return, etc. However, usually the franchisor must approve the buyer. This is because they must make sure that the new buyer will be able to pay their royalties and be at least as successful as you were. The franchisor will likely have net worth requirements and experience specifications for the buyer.

⚜ ⚜ ⚜

Let me tell you more...

One franchisee owned two very successful locations, usually listed in the top ten of all franchisees continually. The owner was a gentleman, not a young man, who decided after several years that he was ready to get out of the business. He listed his locations for sale and found buyers fairly easily, however, the franchisor refused to allow the sales to go through. Logically, the franchisor knew the current franchisee was bringing in lots of royalties and was a sure thing. Allowing the sale opened it up for a new risk for its continued success. The franchisor used the argument that their requirements had changed and they now looked for new owners to have much more net worth than when the current owner signed on.

⚜ ⚜ ⚜

The franchise fee.

The fee you pay that gives you the rights to open a franchise is called the franchise fee. Usually, the first franchise you open is more expensive than the rest. For example, you may pay $40,000 for the rights for the first franchise and then $30,000 for the next five. Each type of business sets its own fees.

Royalties.

Royalties are a percentage of the sales that you do, anywhere from 4 – 11%. There may be additional fees as a percentage of sales, such as advertising or marketing fees, which can be around two percent, but they may not actually call that money "royalties." This fee gives the company more dollars to spend on promoting the business in the media. The franchisor will tell you how they must be paid and when they are due. It is standard to require them to be paid within a week after the previous week's end. Most franchisors will require them to be paid as a withdrawal from your bank account and some may allow you to send them a check. Royalties are seldom waived due to the economy or poor sales and the franchisor may be patient for a while if times are bad, but they will likely sue you for them if you go out of business.

Debiting (automatic bank draft) of royalties is done so that the franchisor gets their money first. This means they have access to your bank account and automatically pull their royalties out of the account when it is due. Over drafting the account or taking out the wrong amount puts you at their mercy. Have a separate account only for royalties and deposit just the right amount to cover what you owe to protect your privacy.

Your net worth.

To open a franchise, you will have to prove to the franchisor that you are financially capable of supporting the business. This means that not only must you show you have the income, the equity or the ability to get a loan to open the business, but they also want to see that you can support the business in an economic downturn. They want to ensure their royalties will be paid, and that they will not have a string of failed franchises around and hurt their reputation. Some businesses will require that you have equity of $1-2 million and others will require much more.

So even if you have the money to open a franchise, you will need much more than that, assuming that the first year or so may be lean.

The Cost of Franchise Ownership

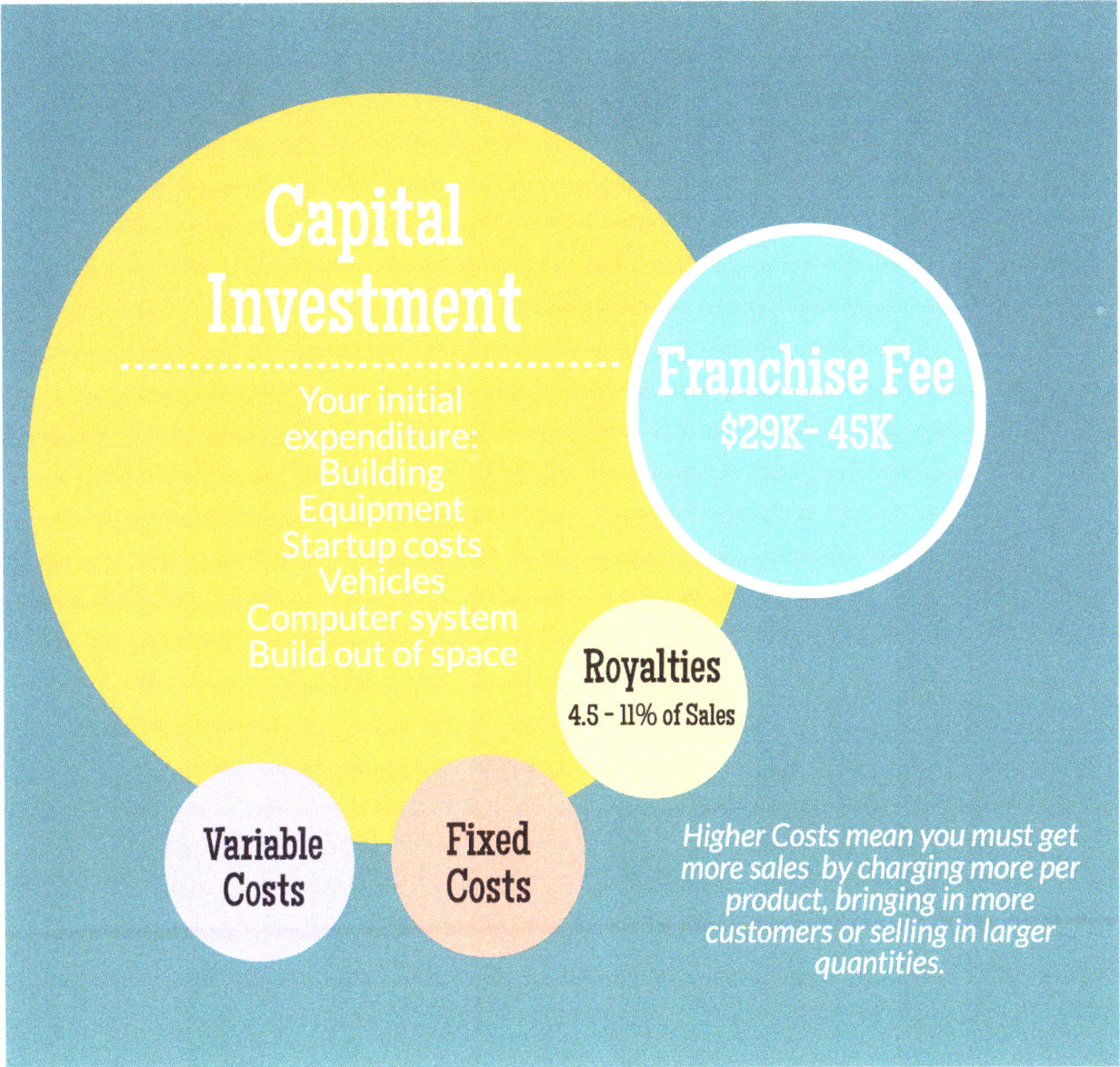

Capital Investment

Your initial expenditure:
Building
Equipment
Startup costs
Vehicles
Computer system
Build out of space

Franchise Fee
$29K - 45K

Royalties
4.5 - 11% of Sales

Variable Costs

Fixed Costs

Higher Costs mean you must get more sales by charging more per product, bringing in more customers or selling in larger quantities.

HUMAN RESOURCES

Good human resource practices.

Any business that hires employees needs to know the labor laws of each state inside and out. Most states require that signs be posted stating the state's minimum wage laws and the current wage. Most states also require an equal opportunity disclosure which summarizes what laws must be obeyed regarding discrimination, sexual harassment, retaliation, hiring employees with disabilities, etc. These signs (usually posters) must be posted in a common area that employees will be able to easily see and read. They are usually available for free from your state. You will often get mail from third party companies that *look* official, telling you that you must order these signs and that you need to pay them a fee. This is just someone out to make money.

New hire documentation.

When hiring employees, you will need to see certain pieces of identification to prove that the person is a citizen or in this country as a legal immigrant or on a work visa. It is the employer's responsibility to look at these documents and determine whether they look real. You are not expected to be an expert in finding forgeries but make a "reasonable effort." If any documents look suspicious, you should not hire the person. Many payroll companies or employee leasing companies (explained later) send the social security numbers through a government database to make sure that they are real. If they are not, then the "new hire" paperwork will be kicked back to you and you will have to ask the employee to correct the documents. This could go on for some time before you finally discover that the documents are not real and the employee cannot be hired.

Interviews.

It is a good idea that when an employee fills out an application, that you have a disclaimer at the end of the application that states that the position is probationary (whatever law exists in your state), that the employee agrees to follow all rules, policies and procedures and that their belongings are open to searches at any time as well as anything else that is important to your business. By having them sign this with the application (keep the signed application!) you have stated certain rights as an employer and they have sworn that they have read and understand the statement.

It is best to have more than one interview with a candidate even if you are desperate for an employee. Some potential employees are able to "fake" it for one interview but their true colors usually come out in more than one. Have other management interview them, also, even if they don't have the decision-making responsibility. Sometimes, an interviewee will disclose something to someone they perceive to be more on their level. Make sure that anyone doing the interviews is aware of all the questions that *are and are not* allowed by law.

There are many questions that you may NOT ask during an interview and to do so can jeopardize your business, even though you may benefit from knowing the information. You cannot ask if anyone has an illness but you CAN ask if there is any reason that they could not lift twenty pounds, which may be a job requirement. You cannot ask about their age or anything that may gives you clues to it, marital status, race, national origin or questions about relatives that might reveal national origin, sexual orientation, if they are a citizen, their health history, if they smoke, how far away they live, religious beliefs, if they have children or intend to get pregnant, whether they own or rent their home, the name of a spouse, details about an arrest if it does not relate to the job, what organizations they belong to and many other questions protected by labor laws.

Some disabilities are specifically protected by law (see the next section). You should always educate yourself and any others in your company that participates in the hiring process so that you completely avoid inappropriate questions. There are legal ramifications for asking the wrong questions and possible financial liability.

Disabilities.

You cannot ask if a person has a disability when interviewing them for a position. You cannot ask a job applicant questions about their health. You can ask them if there is anything that would prevent them from performing the job or if they can lift so many pounds or if they can be on their feet all day, etc. Applicants still have to be able to perform the job they are hired to do, however, certain medical conditions are protected by the Americans with Disabilities Act (ADA). People protected under this act may ask for special accommodations to perform their job AFTER they have been hired. The employer must take steps to allow this along as they can still perform. The employer must not reveal the medical condition to others, unless allowed by the employee.

This can put a small business is a difficult position. Here, it is important to define the job well during the interview or have a written job description. The Disabilities Act requires that you do not discriminate against a person with a handicap or disability; however, the person must still be able to perform the job function. If they are not qualified to do the work, then you are not discriminating against them by not hiring them. A person in a wheelchair will probably not be able to lift fifty pounds over their head. They may be able to sit at a cash register. It all depends on the job requirement.

You must make sure to make every effort to employ the best candidate, even if they have a disability. Those that do may, in return, be more loyal and hard working. It depends on the individual and the circumstances. Some of the specific disabilities covered are epilepsy, paralysis, HIV infection, AIDS, a substantial hearing or visual impairment, mentally challenged, or a learning disability, but short term disabilities such as a broken leg are not. To be defined as a disability, the issue has to affect the person's life. An employer may also be required to make "reasonable accommodations" for the person's disability.

Once they are hired, they can reveal their unknown disability to you and you must work with them. For example, if an employee reveals he has epilepsy and may have a seizure at work, you need to take every precaution to protect the employee from working in a dangerous area or doing anything that can trigger a seizure. However, if the disability prevents him from doing his work, then you need to discipline the employee as you would anyone else.

⚜ ⚜ ⚜

Let me tell you more...

I had three situations where a manager was hired and then told me about a serious health situation. I had a manager voluntarily tell me, after he was hired, that he had epilepsy (protected by ADA) and allowed his fellow employees to know of his condition because of the danger of a seizure. Fellow employees were educated about the warning signs of a seizure so that the manager could be taken to safety or removed from the proximity of equipment that might endanger him. The manager did not experience any seizures while on the job, however, if he had the situation might have endangered not only himself, but those that were trying to assist him. It also means that while the incidence is occurring, no manager would be available to supervise, putting the business in jeopardy, however the owner has no remedy for that according to the law.

⚜ ⚜ ⚜

Felonies on record.

In most states, you have the right to ask if they have any felonies or misdemeanors on the record. You should ask this on the job application so it is in writing. If they lie and you find out they do have a felony, there is immediate grounds for termination of employment. If they state that they do, then a prudent employer will be able to measure the needs for their skills versus the risk you take to employ them. For example, a DUI from twenty years ago may mean little but a recent DUI might mean self control problems, that they may be late to work because they imbibe too much or many other issues. Felonies could be a safety issue for fellow employees and might mean an automatic "no." It all depends on the conviction and what it was for and when.

Payroll taxes.

Many small business owners don't realize that they will have to pay over and above the wages they give their employees to cover payroll taxes. Small businesses usually pay a rate of tax of about 14-16% of gross payroll for federal withholding, Medicare, social security, unemployment tax, state and local income tax, etc. This means that if you pay an employee $8.00 an hour, you are actually paying $9.28 an hour after you figure in the payroll taxes. So, the employee has taxes withheld from his paycheck and you, as the employer also pays taxes on the payroll. However, the employee may get a refund for overpayment of taxes and you will not. The government is *unforgiving* in the filing and paying of payroll taxes. You cannot release your obligation through bankruptcy or other means. You must pay what you owe. Penalties will be charged for late payments and can accrue at a fast rate. This is not something you want to fudge on.

With each payroll, the employer (you) will pay into a fund for unemployment compensation insurance. The larger your payroll, the less you may have to pay so it makes sense to look at using a payroll leasing company to take advantage of lower rates. They bundle all their clients' payrolls together to get a lower rate, but you will still have to pay. The amount you pay can increase when you lay people off and they receive unemployment compensation. For every person that collects this compensation, your rate may increase. That is why employers fight so ferociously to prevent employees who have been fired from being able to collect unemployment by the employee saying they were wrongfully terminated.

Employees that have been fired can still file for unemployment compensation and then you must file a statement that they were *fired*, not laid off. If you actually lay a person off, it is *not* because of their performance, but because you don't have the business to support their job, and they will automatically get unemployment compensation if all other requirements are met (length of service, number of hours worked on average per week, etc.). The fired employee can protest the reason they were fired or say they didn't understand that they were being fired instead of laid off and a hearing will be scheduled. This can take place in person or over the phone with a court mediator listening to both sides and then making a decision as to whether unemployment compensation will be granted.

This situation makes it so vitally important that every time an employee does something against your policy, you document it in their file. If you fire an employee, you should have documentation of every incident of behavior that led to the termination, get any witness statements in writing and place them in the employee's file. The more and better documentation you have will help you prove your case.

Workers compensation.

Workers compensation laws vary from state to state and are designed to protect employees who are injured while on the job. Unfortunately, a lot of abuse of this law occurs when employees realize they may be able to prolong an injury or enhance an injury to receive time off with pay or compensation for pain and suffering. Of course, the real injuries deserve compensation. Worker's compensation is another type of payroll tax and an employer will pay this regardless, and it is usually based on the number of employees and type of claims you have.

In my state, if you have three or fewer employees, it is not required that you must pay for this insurance. For an employee to receive compensation, they must have been injured as a direct result of their employment. If they were on the job where the injury occurred or on an errand at the request of the employer, then it is easy to understand that they deserve compensation. It becomes difficult if they have an injury that is less obvious such as back problems. Employees will have to see a doctor and have a doctor certify their injury and state that it was employment related. The employee will have all medical costs covered and may also receive lost wages. They may have to miss a certain amount of time (such as a week) before they are entitled to lost wages. Permanent handicaps received from an injury can open the door to very large claims of money.

Always be familiar with your own state laws about workers compensation. They can change frequently and it is to your benefit to know every detail. Employees that happen to get "hurt" when out of site of other employees or witnesses or have recurring injuries may need to be reassigned to duties where this cannot happen.

Using a payroll company.

Payroll companies, as opposed to leasing companies, may file your taxes for you and issue payroll checks but they do not have any responsibility in educating you on laws and policies. You directly employ your workers and all the liability is on your shoulders.

Some businesses employ people as a sub-contractor, without deducting taxes from their earnings. *The government does not allow an employer to do this as a means to avoid paying payroll taxes.* Since payroll taxes can add on approximately 14% over and above the actual wage cost, it is a cost savings to pay people as independent contractors. However, you still need to file a 1099 form with the government that shows what you paid to them. The employee is then responsible for paying all his income taxes and no social security tax will be taken out which could hurt them in the long run. You should talk to your accountant if you feel there is a need to pay someone as an independent contractor.

Leasing your employees.

Instead of hiring the employees yourself and handling all the withholding taxes, unemployment taxes, etc. you can use a leasing company for employees. This is not the same as a staffing company that finds employees for you. For a fee, you let the leasing company employ the workers although you do all the legwork of hiring and interviewing; the leasing company files all the paperwork with the government agencies and provides the payroll checks to you to distribute or uses direct deposit into the employees bank account. This does NOT relieve you of following all fair labor practices and laws. You do not have to worry about filing payroll taxes, you get a human resources expert to help walk you through all the legalities concerning hiring and firing, and they may even fill out some of the new hire paperwork for you. Most will also take care of health insurance too.

Make sure you choose a reputable leasing company that can provide you with references and show they have been in business for some time. Because of the serious liability issues of not filing payroll taxes, you need to be absolutely sure that your taxes are being filed and paid for by the leasing company.

An average cost is about 2% of your payroll for the cost to use a leasing company. The employee is "technically" employed by the leasing company, enabling them to take advantage of larger groups and thus receiving lower unemployment compensation and worker's compensation costs. These cost savings should be passed on to you. These companies also file in a timely manner and know exactly what you should do to minimize job injuries and claims. Most of them will have a specialist visit your place of business and look around for any potential problems for injuries. For example, a specialist may look at a restaurant and recommend padded rubber mats where employees stand to reduce fatigue. They may look at the locks on your back door or your security policies to let you know if any changes are necessary to protect your employees from theft.

If you have an employee make a claim, the leasing company will stand by you in letting you know how to handle the claim, let it stand as is or how and when to fight it. If you have an unemployment hearing, a representative from the company should be with you.

Employee handbook.

No matter how small a business you are, you should have an employee manual and make sure the employee has read and signed a statement that they understand it. It should include general statements as to hiring and firing practices, probation, suspension, the scope of the work expected, uniforms, etc. It should also include any information about benefits such as health insurance, vacation and sick leave policies. You can find templates on the Internet.

Most payroll companies have an employee handbook template that you can use. As I was in business longer and longer, the employee manual was revised to reflect situations that were not anticipated at the beginning. An employee brings a water bottle to work filled with vodka? Then write a policy that you have the right to search possessions if you have suspicions of alcohol or using drugs on the job. You suspect someone is stealing money? Write it into your policies that you have the right to ask someone to empty their pockets. Of course, you can't use these policies indiscriminately; you need to have something to back them up, and the longer you are in business, the more situations you may need to cover. It's also a good idea that if you have to take these types of actions, that you have another manager as a witness to what is said and done.

⚜ ⚜ ⚜

Let me tell you more...

If you work with an employee leasing company, it means that technically they employ your employees although you must adhere to all laws. They will maintain all the paperwork and file all the taxes, social security, workers compensation, etc. that you have to pay. They handled health insurance, and other items all for a fee based on a percentage of the payroll. I found it worth it to make sure that a specialist was always handling the legal requirements. I could call with any employee situation and run it by and "expert."

They also provided a basic employee handbook that was customized to create my own manual. It was a great foundation to all the laws of the state; federal and local government and the leasing company also trained all managers on how to comply with the laws. They were able to answer any questions on hiring, firing and discipline that came up. The manual ended up being added to a quite a bit as every new situation that was a "gray" area was then added to the manual.

For example, we allowed only managers to have aprons with pockets. They needed to carry extra pens and magnetic cards to swipe away voids at the registers. They also carried business cards and coupons for those times when they might need to hand them out. We didn't want anyone else to have a pocket conveniently handy when working a cash register since any change due to a customer could be swept into the pocket. If you catch an employee with an apron with pockets and it is NOT covered in the handbook, then you may have to say they were not informed of the policy. If you have it in writing, you can easily discipline them for not following it.

We learned that employees should leave their cell phones in the back of the house where there were employee shelves for their belongings. If that weren't in a written policy, then some employees would be texting whenever they had a moment. If you discipline someone for doing that or they have to be terminated, they may be able to claim that they were never informed of the policy and thus have grounds for unemployment compensation, wrongful termination, etc. If you make sure that on each and every application there is a paragraph that says they have read the Employee Manual and agree to abide by its terms, then they have agreed to comply with all your policies. Doing this on the application covers everyone. Keep all the applications in a file so you can prove they signed it. Keep a manual available for all employees to read or sign out to take home to read.

⚜ ⚜ ⚜

Sample Associate Written Warning Form

Associate Name:_____

Date of Written Warning:_____

Specific rule violation or performance problem:

_____
_____
_____
_____
_____

Previous conversations about the rule violation or performance problem:

_____
_____
_____
_____
_____

Specific change in the associate's performance or behavior that is expected and potential consequences on not meeting expectations:

_____
_____
_____
_____
_____

Associate comments:

_____
_____
_____
_____

Associate Signature:

Supervisor Signature:

Date:

Sample Associate Verbal Warning Form

Associate Name:_____

Date of Verbal Warning:_____

Specific Offense or Rule Violation:

_____
_____
_____
_____
_____
_____

Specific Statement of the expected performance:

_____

_____

_____

Any explanation given by the associate or other significant information:

_____
_____
_____
_____

Associate Signature

Supervisor Signature

Date:

How to
WORK together

Employee Handbook Topics

INTRODUCTION

States facts about the company, that all employees must read and understand the handbook, and a disclaimer that only the owner has to right to change it.

EMPLOYEE RELATIONSHIP

Employment at will
Equal opportunity

COMMENCING EMPLOYMENT

Background checks
Employment status
Probationary period
Job duties
Business' policies
Uniforms
Training

PAYROLL

Working hours & schedule
Timekeeping procedures
Overtime policy
Payment of wages

PERSONNEL

Open door policy
Unlawful harassment
Prohibited conduct
Drug & alcohol abuse
Punctuality & attendance
Background checks
Performance evaluations
Confidentiality
Insider trading policy
Conduct & other employment

FACILITIES

Policy- workplace violence
Operations of vehicles
Use of equipment
Solicitation & distribution of literature
Health & safety

BENEFITS

Holidays
Vacations
Insurance benefits
Leaves of absence

TERMINATION

Voluntary terminations
Involuntary terminations
Reductions in workforce

Change Your Handbook as Your Needs Change!

DON'T MAKE ASSUMPTIONS THAT EMPLOYEES WILL UNDERSTAND WHAT YOU EXPECT. PUT IT IN WRITING.

EMPLOYEE AGREEMENT

ALWAYS have EVERY employee sign and agree to all policies. Place the signed agreement in their employee file.

Exempt employee.

The term "exempt employees" refers to employees that are exempt from overtime. They work on a salary so they work however many hours per week is necessary to get the job done. Non-exempt employees (hourly employees) receive overtime anytime they work more than forty hours per week. They may work more than eight hours in a day but as long as the total hours per week don't go over the normal forty, then overtime need not be paid. State laws can vary so know the laws in your state. Normally, a rate of time and a half is paid for overtime (1.5 times the hourly wage.) Some companies pay even more for employees that work on holidays.

Benefits.

Most full time employees expect benefits. This usually means some type of health care coverage, vacation time, and sick leave. A small company (less than fifty employees) may not have to pay for health care coverage based on the Affordable Care Act but that doesn't mean an employee won't expect health care coverage from you, especially in an environment where getting a good employee onboard is competitive. An employee doesn't necessary see that they are costing you more money. Often, the younger the employee and usually the healthier, they may not care so much about health care coverage but prefer more money in their paycheck. You must check with all state and federal laws to determine if this is legally allowable. Older employees or employees that have health issues will want benefits. You can't ask if they have any issues before you hire them, but once they are on your insurance, you may have to pay higher premiums for employees that smoke or have other health concerns. Check with all state and federal laws to make sure that you follow their guidelines when creating any benefit packages.

Salaried workers will expect a paid vacation. You can make sure that they earn it by accruing time weekly, monthly, etc. If you allow them three sick days per year and they go over the three days, then it can be removed from their vacation *time if you put the benefits package in writing and say this explicitly.* You should always have the employee sign that they understand and reviewed a copy of their benefits handbook. This will prevent future misunderstandings.

Smaller companies will have more difficulty paying for extra types of benefits such as dental insurance, disability insurance and 401K plans. Your profit margins need to be greater to cover your employees in this way and most franchises just don't have the profit for it. Employees should be informed of their "true wage" which includes their wages plus the value of the benefits added on to it so they appreciate the true importance of the benefits they receive.

You can often keep your employees happy by giving them other perks and benefits than just pay. If you're a restaurant, then most employees will likely expect a meal benefit, which may be a reduced price on a meal or a free meal. Often, it is one free or reduced cost meal per shift or per day. Other benefits can include a cell phone paid for by the company or mileage given to an employee that makes a delivery in their personal car. Many employees value the extra things you do for them and it can make their job more fun. You can have employee holiday parties, contests with rewards and the opportunity to make a bonus. Whatever it is, make sure the expectations are set ahead of time. In one business, a woman was hired and told that if she completed a certification program, she would earn a bonus. Afterwards, she was told that the woman who told her about the bonus was no longer with them and had spoken incorrectly. What a demoralizing blow.

✦ ✦ ✦

Let me tell you more...

The Affordable Care Act has changed requirements for small businesses and what the government requires they offer for health care coverage. Small businesses still get to make a log of decisions but if you have over fifty employees you must offer healthcare insurance. If you have fewer than 25 employees you are exempt. To find out the current requirements, visit Healthcare.gov.

✦ ✦ ✦

Drug tests.

You should always reserve the right to drug test any employee. If any behavior appears to be under the influence of drugs or alcohol, you should have a supervisor drive them directly to a clinic that performs drug testing. To make sure that you do not appear to be singling anyone out, you should test more than one person at a time otherwise, if they do not test positive, they can come back and claim they have been discriminated against. Some companies reserve the right to drug test before the person is hired. Many companies have a policy that if an accident occurs on the job, a drug test is mandatory. That could be important in the case of a worker's compensation claim.

✦ ✦ ✦

Let me tell you more...

At one point, I hoped that an employee brought on to oversee the operations would become a partner in future expansion. He had a wealth of industry experience and was passionate about the business. Unfortunately, his perfectionism also alienated many of the employees. I began to notice that the employees seemed to band together and protested any policies or changes he suggested. Having to monitor the situation more closely, directly opposite to the reason he was hired so that I could free up my time, I noticed that he seemed to be slurring some words at times and became aware that he may have a problem with substance abuse.

After having some talks with him, he admitted that he had back pain and often took medication for it. The problem seemed to grow worse and I began to hear about him treating other employees poorly by saying rude things. Observing him one day, after he had to fire an employee (which he did professionally), afterwards he whispered a nasty comment under his breath and several employees heard it.

I talked to him again and he told me just how much medication he was taking and he revealed an addiction. At that point, his ninety-day probation period was over and he either had to be hired or offered an extension. He declined an offered extension, which was given with the stipulation that he get help for his substance abuse, and left the business.

Sexual harassment.

Sexual harassment is a very real issue in many workplaces. Think about the different cultures, different age groups and sexes coming together with different expectations as to friendship, professionalism and their degree of commitment to their job and you are bound to get into the realm of sexual harassment. Sexual harassment encompasses dirty jokes, revealing pictures, using bad language, inappropriate comments, implying that someone must give sexual favors for a promotion or to be hired, asking a person for a date, or even just a glance that makes a person uncomfortable. The recipient of the sexual harassment also has a responsibility to report the incidence to their supervisor. The business owner cannot do anything about it if it is not noticed or reported. Once the incident is reported, then the owner must counsel the perpetrator and insist that it stop. If it recurs, that is when the recipient may be able to make a case that can go to court. It is vitally important that written records be kept of all interviews and actions. You can be held liable.

Depending on the type of sexual harassment, the owner must make a value call on whether the employee actually did what the recipient accused (ask for witnesses to write down their statement), whether it is severe enough to warrant termination, or if a warning will suffice.

Management recruiting.

Making judgments about who should be a manager is an art. Different businesses require different skills, however, all managers need to be able to enforce policies, understand the policies in such a way to be able to use their own judgment, be able to stop negative behaviors, to reinforce positive behaviors, to handle customer complaints, to establish positive relationships with customers, and to represent the company in the best possible light.

Just because someone is a good employee, doesn't mean they will be a good manager or want to be. Management requires certain decision-making skills, confidence, and communication abilities. Many people just don't want the responsibility either or having to be in charge of so many things.

As an employee rises through the ranks, he/she should learn to perform all the jobs in your business. They need to be able to coach and teach others, fill in when needed and set a good example to others. One manager was so good at doing each job that he often had to fill in when someone called out sick and he was already on duty. He was such a huge help that he willingly worked double shifts when necessary and did it with enthusiasm. These kinds of managers are invaluable.

Let me tell you more...

It was planned that two of my managers would eventually help me open more franchises and become partners as we grew. One of the managers had been on board for a while, handling his own store but gradually becoming more and more uncooperative when asked about providing reports or information. One afternoon, the manager had words with me to the degree that I felt he needed to go home to cool off before he said anything he shouldn't. I told him he should go home for a while and we could talk later about his disagreement concerning his job duties. This made him angry and he escalated the conversation, starting to yell at me. I again told him to go home, quit yelling and not to speak to me like that. He told me he could speak to me however he wanted and began to get closer and closer, yelling more directly in my face. By now, I was wondering how to get out of the office since he had me pinned in and if this would escalate to physical violence. Finally, he threw his office keys down on the desk and yelling, "I quit," stomped out of the office. Of course, the other manager that was to be a partner had to pick up the slack, working at two locations and helping to hire a new manager. The manager that got stuck with more work didn't complain and did her best, and yes, it was the guy's wife.

One of my general managers was with me for about a year and had worked his way up the ranks. He was now in charge of one restaurant. He did an adequate job and was paid very well. Whenever any employee begins to act differently or will not make eye contact, it's obvious something is up. The general manager did not respond with any issues when I tried to casually ask him how things were going. One day, with a junior manager in the store, the manager threw his keys down on the office table, exited the building, jumped in his truck and floored it out of the parking lot as if his tail was on fire. All this was observed on the cameras when it was watched later. After finding the keys in the office, the junior manager looked at the cameras and saw that the other manager "had given his notice."

Although you always hope that anyone giving supervisory responsibilities will exercise good judgment, some things happen that are based on a lack of maturity levels. I had a young man responsible for the closing shift when he was twenty years old. He knew his duties well, was smart and good with the customers. It wasn't until after he left that I found out that he and one of the other employees were leaving the building and having sex in his car, on the evening shift. No employee wanted to be the one to spill the beans so I wasn't able to do anything about it after the fact. It was very frustrating to know that my restaurant was being left unsupervised and that he was still earning his wage while using his time to have sex.

⚜ ⚜ ⚜

Accountability.

As a small business owner, you will not be able to make every decision but must entrust certain decisions to your employees. Managers need to be able to handle any situation that occurs when you are not there, even if it is calling you to let you know what is going on. If they cannot reach you, they must handle the situation on their own. Only by discussing possible situations, training and role-playing will the managers learn what your wishes are.

For example, if the fire marshal should walk into your business to perform an inspection, you would want to know immediately that he is there. Your employee should stay with him and take notes as to anything the marshal finds that needs to be changed. You would want to make sure that the employee is polite and respectful. Any violations could shut down your business or mean a return visit so this requires that your manager knows how to make decisions in a split minute as to what to do.

A manager needs to know how much authority he has. Managers need to be held accountable but also need to have some wiggle room to use authority. They have to make decisions quickly while not being so fearful that they will lose their job that they have "analysis paralysis". A manager that makes a poor decision should be coached as to what other avenues were open to them and as to why they didn't choose them. Experience can be a great educator.

Let me tell you more...

There is no one that will treat your business exactly the same as you do, no matter how much they are trustworthy, no matter how much you pay them. Unless someone has put their own money, sweat and tears into a business, they will not make the same decisions that you do.

One day, I went to deposit the cash receipts at the bank about ten minutes away. The restaurant was being managed by an experienced General Manager as well as a regular manager, both seasoned veterans of the restaurant industry. One of the managers thought she smelled natural gas, the other didn't. Since the industrial ovens ran on gas, this could be a serious issue. They asked all the other employees and only one other thought they smelled anything unusual. They called me and I told them I would be there in five minutes and would check it out, since it obviously was not an emergency as the majority of people couldn't discern anything out of the ordinary. I told them to open the doors, just in case.

On my way out of the bank parking lot, I was passed by several fire engines with their lights and sirens on. With a sinking heart, I arrived at my restaurant to find all the firefighters pulling off their gear and rather disgustedly saying there was no problem.

I asked the managers what had happened and the one that thought she smelled gas had called the fire department "just to inquire" how to find out if we had a leak. Of course, no fire department could fail to respond to that kind of situation and called it in as an emergency. The manager didn't wait for my arrival and took action that put the sales of the restaurant in jeopardy. Now, if there really had been a problem then perhaps she did the right thing, but most businesses only get so many false alarms before the county invoices them for the trouble of sending emergency personnel when there is no issue.

Employee courtesies.

Most employees will react better to a question than a command. No one likes to think they have to take orders. Employees usually appreciate that they "may" have an implied choice although the right choice is to do what is asked of them.

As long as everyone has the expectation to be treated with respect, the culture of the company will be one where people feel valued. Once an employee is yelled at, rather than counseled, their feeling of humiliation will continue to fester. There is always a calm, collected way to say anything, even a criticism. Every employee should be able to feel that they have certain courtesies due to them.

Clocking in and out.

Most Point of Sale (POS) systems will have a way for an employee to clock in and out of his shift. Salaried employees usually do not clock in and out because it is assumed they will be on the job until the job is done, however, if you really want to keep track of who is on the premises, it is wise to have *everyone* clock in and out. Each employee is assigned a code that they use at a point of sale register to perform this task. The payroll/point of sale system will then print out labor reports that will show you how many hours each employee worked and if there was any overtime.

Since overtime is paid at a higher rate so it is important to monitor this daily. As you see an employee approaching overtime, you may need to switch around employee schedules to prevent this higher cost.

An employee that continually clocks in before his/her shift will cost you money. If an employee clocks in fifteen minutes early five shifts per week at $10 per hour they have cost you $14.25 (allowing for payroll taxes). If you want them on the job early, that is one thing, but to have them sipping coffee on the clock is like paying them to be unproductive. Over the course of a year, this amounts to $741. Now, imagine more than one employee doing this and see what it does to your labor cost.

An employee that continues to "forget" to clock in and out creates havoc with labor cost reports. It also means you must estimate when they were on the job and off so that you will not know for sure if you are paying them the correct amount. They should be verbally warned with progression to written warnings if it continues to happen with all verbal and written warnings fully documented. Never allow another employee to clock someone else in. No employee should ever know another employee's code. Friends may cover for friends and you may find yourself paying someone that wasn't really on the job.

If you don't have a POS system, then a validated way to record time cards should be used. Even a small thing such as requiring employees to use a pen and not a pencil that can be erased later, is a smart thing to do. They should be required to initial the in/out times.

Remember that even small amounts of time can amount to big dollars if allowed to continue on unchecked.

Employee Time Card And Job Detail

| Period From : 12/26 | To : 01/08 | | | | Printed on Monday, January 09 | | 10:15 AM |

Employee # And Name		Payroll ID				
Luke - Summary		30 - Staff				
Total Hours Worked This Pay Period:	61.32	61.32	499.76	0.00	499.76	459.90

134 - Zachary

Job # and Name	Clock In/Out Date and Time		Hours	Status	Adjusted By	Reason
30 - Staff	IN Mon	12/26/2005 3:49pm		No Schedule		
	OUT	5:04pm	1.25	Mgr Clock Out		
30 - Staff	IN Tue	12/27/2005 3:44pm		No Schedule		
	OUT	5:39pm	1.91	No Schedule		
30 - Staff	IN Tue	12/27/2005 6:09pm		No Schedule		
	OUT	9:21pm	3.20	No Schedule		
Total Hours Worked This Week:			6.36	Regular: 6.36	Overtime: 0.00	
30 - Staff	IN Tue	1/3/2006 3:55pm		No Schedule		
	OUT	5:37pm	1.71	No Schedule		
30 - Staff	IN Tue	1/3/2006 6:08pm		No Schedule		
	OUT	9:40pm	3.53	No Schedule	Bob A.	On Time
30 - Staff	IN Wed	1/4/2006 5:12pm		No Schedule		
	OUT	5:49pm	0.61	No Schedule		
30 - Staff	IN Wed	1/4/2006 6:20pm		No Schedule		
	OUT	9:36pm	3.27	No Schedule	Gail B.	On Time
30 - Staff	IN Thu	1/5/2006 4:25pm		No Schedule		
	OUT	7:31pm	3.09	No Schedule		
30 - Staff	IN Thu	1/5/2006 8:02pm		No Schedule		
	OUT	9:34pm	1.54	No Schedule	Matt K.	On Time
Total Hours Worked This Week:			13.75	Regular: 13.75	Overtime: 0.00	

Job Totals	30 - Staff	Regular Hours	Overtime Hours	Regular Pay	Overtime Pay	Total Pay
	20.11	20.11	0.00	161.88	0.00	161.88
Total Hours Worked This Pay Period:	20.11	20.11	0.00	161.88	0.00	161.88

> The employee forgot to clock in three times and a manager had to adjust the time card.

136 - Mary

Job # and Name	Clock In/Out Date and Time		Hours	Status	Adjusted By	Reason
30 - Staff	IN Tue	12/27/2005 4:35pm		No Schedule		
	OUT	9:30pm	4.92	No Schedule		

Special protection for teenagers.

There are also additional laws that protect younger workers. Most states will say how many hours a day a teen can work and at what ages, when they need to take a break and how long it must be. Any business can be audited to be sure they are following the law so proper documentation must be kept to show when teens clocked in to work, their break time and length, as well as the time they left for the day. The laws set a curfew on nights that teens work if the following day is a school day. Often, the laws for this are void if the teen is emancipated or married. If the business owner has a child that works in the family business, the laws are often voided also. It is up to the parent to set the hours and the type of work the child does as long as he/she is not endangered.

Getting the attention of the labor board can mean probation for your business, random checks from a labor board representative and fines. Any time a labor board representative visits your business they will require you to show proof of all employee time cards, labor reports and valid proof of their age. In my state, minors can only work for four hours at a time without a break. *This does not mean four hours and one minute.* A violation can be subject to a $10,000 fine.

You may find that some minors desperately need money and will want to work longer hours, but you cannot let them because of the labor laws. You may find that some of them do not take their full break or their lunch or dinner hour, hoping to gain as much time on the clock as possible. Some POS systems will not let a minor clock back in to work if they have not taken the full time they must, which is a great safeguard. If you do not have that system, you must strictly enforce the rules.

Most laws protect anyone under the age of eighteen from handling dangerous chemicals even if it is a necessary part of the job. In my state, a teen may not fill a sanitizer bottle in a restaurant with the chemicals although they are allowed to clean a table with a spray bottle containing the sanitizer. Teens may also not use any dangerous machinery such as a meat slicer or even a bagel slicer. In an environment where many teens work at night, a business must make sure that there is at least one eligible person available to handle chemicals and machinery.

Employing minors means you need to follow more stringent requirements for labor laws, but having a mix of ages working for you can mean a greater sense of community. Minors bring a sense of enthusiasm and high energy. Many teenagers are very bright and can be a real asset. Finding a teen that is responsible and likeable to your customers will be a hit. Customers usually respect a young person working hard to do a good job.

⚜ ⚜ ⚜

Let me tell you more...

In my state, to start a labor investigation into any business, an *anonymous* caller can claim they saw an underage worker being taken advantage of. The caller does not have to leave their name or any other information to prove it is a legitimate claim. Also in my state, it is legal for a business owner to use their children to work at younger ages. Having my twelve year old son work as a greeter at the store (something he loved to do) was a lot of fun for him and the customers, too, especially the older ones who missed their grandkids. Many friendships were started between my son and my customers.

One of the other teenage employees resented that he had to work with my son who would occasionally work behind the counter too. The only reason for it was that my son knew more about the business than the employee and the employee had an ego. I can't prove it was him, but someone called the labor board and claimed that I was taking advantage of an underage employee. This caused the board to send a representative and I had to prove to them all the ages of my employees, if I couldn't, there was the possibility of a $10,000 fine. I had all the documents but it took hours to copy them and put them together so the representative could look at them. After the interview, it was obvious that only my son was too young to be employed and he was exempt from any problem. However, since they had opened a case, they would not close it without several more visits where they again repeated all the paperwork and took up hours more of my time and wasted our taxpayer's dollars.

Breaks for employees.

In many states, breaks for adults are not required, however, treating your employees right pays off. It is common courtesy to make sure an employee's needs are met with time for a break, to use the restroom, or to eat. Some employees will need their break time to run to the bank or to their child's school. As long as the privilege is not abused, allowing the employee to take care of their needs usually means a hard working, loyal employee. Some employees will prefer to work through break times because they need the money. This means it is a decision for your labor cost as to whether you want to allow this or not.

Different views of employees.

Most employees will not fully understand the labor laws in your state. Some will think that a common practice such as taking a break is actually a law and when they don't get their break for some reason, feel as if the business has broken the law. It may be to your benefit to explain the labor laws to your employees if you are usually more generous than the law. For example, if breaks aren't required, but you want to take care of your employees and give them a break, then let them know this is a benefit that you are giving them, and not the law.

Adhering to the IRS.

An owner that actively works in the business may need to pay himself a salary, even if the company is set up as an "S" corporation where all the profits flow into the owner's personal income tax returns. The reason a salary may still be required has to do with social security taxes. The federal government still wants to make sure that you are contributing. You should check with your accountant about this but beware this may be required. This means that you will have to pay payroll taxes on your own salary so much less is actually going into your own pocket out of your own profits. Assume you pay yourself $50,000 for running the business. You would see the deduction for payroll taxes out of the paychecks so you might only be taking home $35,000 and then in addition to that reduction, you will have to pay the employer's portion of payroll taxes; another 13-16%, so you just laid out another $7500. Doing the math, you just lost a chunk of change for paying yourself.

An owner should never attempt to avoid paying their share of taxes since this could be the basis for an audit. You should pay yourself a salary and allow taxes to be deducted so that you follow federal standards.

Referrals.

When you have a really great employee and they refer a friend or family member to you, it is great to think that by hiring their friend you will give them some reason to stick with you. However, the opposite is true. Now if the friend or family member becomes unhappy with you or is fired, then you may lose the good employee, too.

Even a good employee can become distracted by having a friend working with them, so be cautious. If the friend looks like a good employee on their own merits, then you can always try to keep the two working on different shifts. You may also want to set some boundaries immediately, letting them know that they cannot have special privileges just because they are friends.

Employee reviews.

When you hire an employee, you should let them know what your review policy is. Do they get a review once a year or more frequently? Can they expect a yearly raise? What is the criteria for a raise? Employees come from all different types of experiences and some may expect frequent job evaluations and some may not. Most employees expect a raise in wage along with a review. Not meeting an employee's expectations can lead to a disgruntled employee.

If you promise an employee that you will give them a review or evaluation, then do it in a timely manner. Making an employee wait can really make them unhappy.

Make sure that reviews are done in privacy where no other employee will hear what you say. The review should be formalized, in writing, and kept in the employee's file. A rating system is best, one that is simple but yet will describe the employee's job progression, performance and adherence to policies. It can be as easy as "exceeds expectations, meets expectations, or needs improvement." It can be a rating system such as a 1-5 scale. Whatever you choose, make it consistent and easy to understand across the board. An employee that doesn't understand what is expected with his/her goals will lose interest and stop trying.

Probationary period.

If you are unsure whether to hire someone and your state has a probationary period allowed, then you can always bring someone on at one wage with the understanding that if they perform well, you will hire them on permanently at a higher rate. This gives you the opportunity to try them out while they know they have to work hard to make the grade. This can be a win-win situation. In cases where an employee doesn't have a good reference or doesn't have much experience in your industry, this trial period can be very effective.

In my home state, the probation period is ninety days so if it looks like an employee will not work out, you should let them go within this time period. It's just easier. You can also put in writing that you are extending the probation period as long as the employee agrees to it and signs off on it. Then, you have more time to decide if the employee should be kept on. Every employee should have well defined job responsibilities and know exactly what is expected to get a higher wage.

Right to work states.

As mentioned above, some states are called "right to work" states. The state has a law that says that anyone can be fired or let go at any time for whatever reason. This gives the mistaken assumption that you can treat an employee poorly, for this is not true. You still have to follow all the rules you have set up for probationary periods, sanctions, and disciplinary action. You must absolutely document and have witnesses for all your actions. This law does not excuse poor behavior or harassment of any kind. It does, however, give you some leeway in the reasons that the employee is being let go.

Training period.

A training period is one of the most valuable times you have. Often, you are under the gun and need a warm body immediately, so that the employee must get thrown into the activities quickly. You should view the training time as an investment. The more time and effort spent in doing it correctly gives you a greater return in employee productivity, efficiency, better satisfied customers and employee loyalty. No one enjoys feeling as if they are doing something wrong, so the better you train someone, the more confidence they will have. It is also a time to bond with management. The employee will get to know people on a more personal level and begin to form bonds.

⚜ ⚜ ⚜

Let me tell you more...

I had one employee who was very ambitious but English was his second language. It was always difficult to tell just how much he understood since he often repeated the same mistakes, but he tried hard. I ended up hiring an English tutor and allowed him to take lessons for about six weeks to determine if he was able to move forward or not. It turned out that the problem was not the language but his understanding of business. I was able to determine that he was not a good prospect for management since the issue was not language, but knowledge and skills.

⚜ ⚜ ⚜

Updating employee records.

It's important to make sure an employees know he has a responsibility to update his address with his employer at all times. Sometimes, an employee is fired or quits and doesn't leave his new address. If that happens, his final paycheck may sit in the company safe because some payroll companies require that the last paycheck be *mailed* and not direct deposited. State laws come into play here, but it is important that you are able to contact an ex-employee and provide them with their rightful pay.

Setting expectations.

In most states you have the right to ask if an employee can physically perform the work. This may mean that you have to decide if they might need to lift twenty pounds when a delivery is made or if they need to carry items to re-stock shelves. It's best to know upfront if they can do this or not because if they say they can, but then cannot perform the duties, you have a right to fire them because they lied about their capabilities. If they told you at the start that there may be difficulties, and you hired them anyway, they may have a case against you for wrongful termination. The point is, cover your bases at the beginning of a new hire, don't think you can change things half way through. Most employees will not mind, but some will want to take you to the cleaners so you need to have policies in place to protect yourself from the few.

Handling tips.

Tips. In almost any business, there may be a situation where a customer likes one of your employees so much that they give them a tip. You need to decide ahead of time, if you will allow the employee to keep all of the tip or if there is a joint container where tips are pooled for all employees. If an employee is handed the tip but doesn't get to keep it, they may feel upset to have to share it. If however, you only have a few employees that actually work with customers and there are a lot of support personnel behind the scenes then it may make sense to have their share.

Rewarding the best.

Everybody these days is very sensitive to discrimination, and rightfully so. As a business owner, you must make sure that everyone is treated fairly. It is difficult to treat everyone "equally" because all employees are not created equally. You will have those employees that just want to put in their time and take home a paycheck and those employees that put their heart and soul into their jobs. The employees that work harder usually receive more leeway and obtain privileges. Privileges can range from getting holidays off or being the first to choose the shift they want.

Others may see this as discrimination against them. You must always know what is real discrimination and what is part of having a business. You can never discriminate on the basis of race, religion, culture, marital status, sexual orientation, etc. but you can give the best employees promotions and privileges.

When employees don't live up to expectations.

We would all like to think that we are great managers or that most employees really know how to work, but many employees come from backgrounds where self-discipline has not been valued. Some employees may find it hard to arrive at work on time, may have a tendency to want to talk on their cell phones or do other things that are not productive and you, as a business owner, don't want to have to pay them for. If you have fully communicated their job responsibilities to them and have given them some type of education to correct negative behaviors and that still hasn't worked, then it is time for progressive discipline.

Progressive discipline means that the more an employee does something against policy, the more punitive measures are used. For example, if someone arrives late for work repeatedly, you may have to cut their shift by an hour (i.e. they make less money) to send them a message. If that doesn't work, then you may have to cut out an entire day's shift. All of their actions should, again, be documented. If you find them repeatedly standing around, then they need to be assigned more and more tasks to keep them busy. You will usually reach a "critical" point where you find that their effort either doesn't make their wages worthwhile or that their services just aren't benefitting you. Then you have to make the decision of whether to just cut their hours way back or let them go. You should have this as a written policy in the employee handbook.

When an employee is continually late, find out if there is a cause such as a childcare issue or a bus schedule problem. If you can work around this for a good employee, it is usually worth it. If it is truly a problem with the employee not being to arrive on time because of their own scheduling abilities, then they may need to be moved to another time slot. It all boils down to whether the annoyance is worth it to keep a good employee. Are there others waiting to take their place? Can they be trained to arrive earlier? Does their late arrival set a bad example? Does the practice disrupt business?

⚜ ⚜ ⚜

Let me tell you more....

At times, even the best employees will experience upheaval in their private lives. Most often, people can still perform their jobs, even if in a diminished state albeit temporarily. Sometimes, an employee will bring their issues into the workplace and then cause a disruption more far reaching. A manager, going through a divorce, was emotionally upset for weeks. She used her fellow employees as a sounding board to recount her arguments and disputes with her spouse. Because she was well liked, everyone was sympathetic and listened. Deciding how long to let this kind of thing go on or whether you nip it in the bud and let the employee know that this kind of behavior is not allowed is more of an art than a science. On one hand, it is disruptive to the business; on the other hand if she doesn't let out some of the stress of the situation, she may not be able to perform her job *at all* and may end up being fired. The cost to hire and train a new manager is expensive. This is a time where verbal counseling may be required. Guidance as to when it is appropriate to discuss her issues (on breaks, after work hours, before work, etc.) may help. If the discussions continue, then progressive action is necessary such as written warnings, which can make you seem unsympathetic to the rest of your employees.

⚜ ⚜ ⚜

Firing.

Firing an employee requires previous documentation of each and every occurrence of a policy violation and this policy needs to be followed equally for all employees so that no one employee can claim discrimination.

When you fire someone, you want to make sure that you have documentation that cannot be questioned. Always put warnings in writing. Stick to a policy of so many warnings means an employee gets fired. When you fire someone, if at all possible, have a witness there to make sure they can back you up if the employee files for unemployment compensation and says they weren't really fired, but just laid off. It is always important to have two managers present when firing an employee, one to speak to the employee and one to act as a witness. A fired employee does not collect unemployment compensation unless they can prove unjust cause. As a business owner, the more employees that get unemployment compensation, the higher your tax will be and the less money you will make.

It is especially important if the employee is expected to be angry or upset. Having a third party as a witness will help later on if the employee makes statements that are not true. It will also help document what was said to the employee and show that they were truly fired and not laid off.

⚜ ⚜ ⚜

Let me tell you more...

I had a five-year employee who was increasingly frustrated with his work. He had learned many different positions and had maxed out on what new jobs he could learn because of his customer skill level. He had difficulty dealing with people face to face and so was placed in jobs that were in the back end of the restaurant. He began to tell people he wanted out which is not good for morale and then he began to say things, sometimes under his breath, sometimes disrespectful and sometimes a bit lewd. He would not come out and just quit but it seemed he wanted to be fired. I believed that he didn't want to tell his wife he quit since he probably needed the job.

He continued to escalate his behavior until it was disruptive and he had to be fired. Afterwards, he filed a grievance and I was required to do a phone interview with him and a labor representative on the line. I had used a manager as a witness to the firing so that if there were any problems the manager could tell his version of what happened too. The ex-employee was allowed to have another person with him listening to help him understand the conversation. The ex-employee used his mother, which made me uncomfortable having to re-tell some of the things the employee had said (especially the lewd parts). The labor representative required that I tell her all of it and afterwards found that he had no basis for the grievance.

⚜ ⚜ ⚜

Cobra.

Cobra is the government's answer to allowing an employee to keep their health insurance after they are laid off or lose a job. If your give your employees health benefits, then after they leave it is up to them to work with the insurance company and pay for Cobra benefits out of pocket.

Employee grievances.

If an employee objects to being fired, they will file a grievance. You will be contacted usually through a letter explaining that the employee has done so. You will then be asked to file some paperwork explaining why the employee was fired, how it was done and supply any documentation you have. Documentation will usually consist of any warnings in the employee's file, written and signed statements from other employees or managers that witnessed negative behaviors, and progressive discipline or warnings that were carried out.

If the state believes there still may be doubt, then a hearing will be scheduled. Both the employer and the employee will be at the hearing either in person or via the phone. Both sides will tell their story to a mediator and then the mediator will inform the employee and the employer of their decision for future action. If the mediator finds that the employer was justified in firing the employer, then the former employee receives no unemployment compensation. If he opposite occurs, the employee may receive the compensation or other damages, depending on state laws. Some employees may be entitled to get their job back or receive back wages.

You may think that you have an open and shut case of terminating an employee but by the time the employee tells their story to a third party, it may be open to interpretation. That is why it is so vitally important to document negative behaviors and put warnings in writing.

⚜ ⚜ ⚜

SAFETY AND SECURITY

Security for everything.

Security is an integral part of any business. It means providing a secure and safe working environment, protecting private information of employees such as their social security number, protecting *your* private information from access *by* your employees, making sure your money is safe, your computer data is safe, that any customer or vendor has a safe, secure experience, and making sure that you have an emergency plan in case of severe weather, or other disasters.

Your building should be secure. This means adequate deadbolts on all doors and security cameras in place. Security systems can now be monitored over the Internet so you can watch what is going on in your business while you sit at home. If an employee leaves your business and has had a key to the premises, then the locks should always be re-keyed as a matter of policy.

Having an alarm system that is monitored by a security company is a good idea. Panic alarms should be placed in areas where robbers tend to isolate employees such as the freezer or walk in cooler in a restaurant. Panic alarms should also be in the office and near the cash registers. They operate by using two buttons, which will both have to be pressed at the same time, to send an alarm directly to the police. This will cause a silent alarm and no siren will sound but the police will be immediately dispatched without the security monitoring company calling the business first.

Smoke detectors are required and should also be monitored by a security company. Most public building codes will also require a sprinkler system in case of fire.

Providing security is not enough, you also have to be extremely careful to make sure that your building is safe in every way. You need to make sure people can't trip. You must put out "wet floor" signs if it rains or if the floor is mopped. You must make every effort to ensure that every person, whether employee, vendor or customer, is as safe as possible at every moment of the day. You cannot leave cleaning chemicals anywhere a child could get hold of them. You must watch out for hinges that close doors too hard or fast.

⚜ ⚜ ⚜

Let me tell you more...

It is always a touchy balance between keeping your customers happy and making sure that the children they are letting run around your business, are safe. You may insult the customers if you come right out and ask them to rein in the kids, but you might also be the target of a lawsuit if you don't make sure they stay safe. Parents may have unrealistic expectations of what a business should do or can do to protect the kids. Kids don't read warning signs for wet floors, they don't know that a swinging door can hit them from behind, they don't know that a piece of equipment may be hot because they haven't experienced life yet. Parents are supposed to monitor their children but in our society, that doesn't always happen. As a business owner, you must be careful to keep everyone comfortable too, and some customers will be very frustrated with kids running around and making noise. Sometimes it's a value judgment on whom you want to come back and what you want to say. You have the right to refuse service to anyone but can you accept the ill will you might generate?

If you are a business that offers free Wi-Fi to customers you need to also have convenient electrical outlets so customers can re-charge their devices. If not, they will run their own extension cords to reach an outlet, which could cause another customer to trip. As unbelievable as it is, the customer that plugged in the extension cord is often disgruntled when you ask them to unplug it because of customer safety. You are ultimately responsible for what happens in your building and you are the one that will get sued if you don't make sure the every customer is protected. One computer user plugged in his electrical cord right by the food pick up station and stretched it across the aisle at about twelve inches off the ground, just the right height for a "trip wire."

⚜ ⚜ ⚜

Security

For Your Business

Tip: Vary the times of the day you take cash to the bank. Don't use signage on your car. Don't carry money bags.

1
Cameras should be placed throughout so there are no "dead-spots"

2
Have an alarm system connected to all windows, doors and ceiling accesses

3
Don't leave your back door open or unlocked. Make employees ring a bell for entrance

4
Have panic alarms

5
Keep your office locked and your safe hidden and secure

6
Protect all your data: yours, the employees' and customers'

Tip: Having a TV screen just inside your back door hooked up to an exterior camera and light helps you to see who is at the door in the dark.

Protecting credit cards.

By law, all credit card information most be protected against theft. This means that if you run credit cards over an Internet line for approval, you must not retain any information that can be found and used by others. This is due to identity theft and the opportunity of hackers getting credit card numbers and using them or selling them. You must have a firewall on your computer to protect anyone from monitoring your data transmissions to the credit card company when you swipe a card to get the approval for it.

It used to be that you could store a person's credit card number on your computer. That way, if a customer disputed a charge or asked why you charged their card, you could look up the credit card number on reports. Because of the security issues with credit cards now and the change in the law, you can no longer keep the full data but only a small part of it. It makes it much more difficult to find information if a customer disputes a charge, however, there is not much you can do about that. For example, a customer sees that his credit card statement or bank account has been charged by your business, then he calls your establishment to tell you he didn't buy anything. You cannot search your computer by his credit card number to find the transaction. You will have to search by the amount he was charged and then try and match a name or the last four digits of the credit card, or whatever information your computer stores. Sometimes, you will not be able to find the transaction and without proof, he can get out of paying you. That is also why you should keep a duplicate copy of the receipt for as long as your credit card processor recommends. You may have to physically go through receipts to match up the amount, name and last four digits of the credit card but at least you will have proof that you can present to the credit card processor as well as the customer. This is a laborious process.

Cash handling threats.

In any business where there is a lot of cash, cash-handling safety is extremely important. Most businesses use a heavy-duty floor safe to store cash deposits. Only a limited number of employees (usually with manager level responsibility) should have access. Some businesses will use a "deposit" safe where the closing manager deposits the cash and only the owner of the business can open it. If an employee leaves your employ and knows the code, change it, if possible. Also, make sure you receive their keys back and if you feel there is any risk, re-key your locks. It gets expensive, but not as expensive as losing a deposit.

Although floor safes may weigh a few hundred pounds, leave it to the industrious to figure out ways to get them out of a building. One restaurant in the same chain had a thief access their safe from a door in the roof, haul it through the doorway and it somehow ended up in a shopping cart being wheeled down the street when the thief was apprehended.

Any business that deals with cash needs to take measures against theft including the threat of a robbery from the outside, theft or embezzlement from an employee and even from a customer. Cash must be protected while in the cash register drawer, when moving from the safe to the front of the business cash register system, while in the safe, and when making a deposit.

How does one steal money when he/she is an employee? If the POS system is computer oriented, then the cash register will accrue all sales and the amount of cash sales versus credit sales. So, when you want to pull out a cash drawer to count it and make sure all the cash is there, you first run a report on the register and that will tell you exactly how much cash you should have in the drawer. If there are any shortages, then you must find out how many people used the cash register. There are benefits to assigning only one person to using a particular cash drawer but this may be impractical in high activity environments or where the cashier has to leave his station to retrieve a product for a customer and another employee must use the register. To totally hold one employee responsible for any missing cash, you would have to count the cash drawer at both the beginning and end of their shift and make sure no one else was allowed on the register. Theft may not be the only reason cash is missing, poor counting is another reason. Someone has to be held accountable for the money in a cash drawer. Sometimes, the cashier must also count the money and they may have to make up any shortages.

One way a cashier can circumvent the system is to steal money from the customer's change. This can work in very busy environments where the customer is less likely to count their change. The cashier removes the customer's change from the cash drawer and then palms a dollar, letting it slide into their pocket while handing the rest of the change to the customer so it is the customer who is shorted and not the cash drawer.

Anyone with a code or magnetic card, which allows one to override the cash register POS system, can also steal. Usually, only a manager is allowed to override the system. A manager should never give out his code or card or allow an employee that does not have a magnetic card to use his. It may seem fine to allow a trusted employee to use the code or card; however, at some point the employee may become disgruntled and can do a lot of damage with this knowledge. Whoever has access to an override code or card can void out a sale, even though it took place. That means that cash could be removed from the drawer without the computer catching the error. You should make sure that each manager has a different override code so a void can be tracked back to the manager by his/her code. Most computers will print out a report of the times when voids are made and what code made them. Make sure to check it often to look for patterns that might be suspicious. If there is adequate time, ask the cashier for an explanation of why they need a void. If customers are waiting in line, this may not be appropriate but should be reviewed later.

Another way that an employee can steal is to give away products and services for free to friends or other employees without ringing up the sale on the cash register. There should also be an override code required for discounts (which can be hectic during peak times) but without the code, an employee can't give discounts to friends. They should have to ask a manager.

A safe should be counted several times a day if managers are removing change from it. Any shortages should be identified immediately. A log should be kept to see when shortages occurred and what manager was on duty. Look for patterns.

If a manager is the one to put together a cash deposit, consider a safe that allows the deposit to slide into the safe through a slot and that cannot be opened other than by the owner. This means that no one can tamper with the deposit once it has been accumulated and holds that particular manager liable for the integrity of the deposit.

Transporting cash deposits to the bank should be made with care. Using a money bag is like having a target on your back. Vary the times you visit the bank and consider a money transporting service, which can be rather expensive, if safety is a concern. Anytime you deposit more than $10,000, the government requires a form with all your information on it to validate that the money came from a business transaction and not from money laundering or illegal activities. Making a cash deposit should only be done by a very trusted employee or the owner. There are lots of stories out there of a manager just one day walking away with a several thousand-dollar deposit. Yes, you may catch them and prosecute, but will you get your money back? If the deposit is taken to the bank, it can be deposited in a night depository or in person during the day. If you leave it in the depository, then you will not know until later if there was a discrepancy on the deposit ticket from the actual cash. The bank will most likely charge you a fee if they determine that the deposit slip and the actual amount are different. By depositing the amount in person you will know immediately if there is an issue.

You should make it a point to vary your routine when going to the bank. You do not want anyone to know that at a certain time every day you will be walking to your car with cash. Be aware of your surroundings and be watchful of other customers at the bank, also. Once they learn you are a business owner, they may pay more attention to you.

Anytime someone other than you as a business owner handles cash, you expose yourself to the risk of mistakes in making change, mistakes in counting, theft which can include giving too much change in a cash transaction to "friend," pocketing money, or supposed losses to a scam artist.

The fewer the number of people that handle the money the better. The more audit trails you have to track money as well as systems set up for protection the better. All sums of money should always be kept in a safe that is also behind a locked door, if possible. It should not be visible to multiple employees, vendors or customers. People who handle money as part of their business can end up getting so used to it as part of their daily routine, that they open themselves to mistakes and theft. Always be aware of who sees the money and what safeguards are in place.

The money that is used to handle cash sales on a daily basis should be kept in a safe at a standard amount. For example, if you know that you will be using fifty dollars worth of pennies, fifty dollars worth of dimes, etc. then establish a par or standard for the exact amount that will be kept in the safe at all times. As those rolls of coins are used by being transferred to a cash register drawer for change, then they should be "bought" by dollar bills out of the register drawer. So, even if the amount of pennies drops to twenty dollars, if the par is fifty dollars in pennies, then there should be another thirty dollars in bills to make up for the usage in the pennies.

All cash register drawers should be kept with a standard amount of change in them. If you decide that you need $200 in change, you may want to keep fifty dollars in quarters, ten dollars in dimes, two dollars in nickels, one dollar in pennies, eighty dollars in twenties, twenty dollars in tens, twenty dollars in fives and seventeen dollars in ones. Knowing your "par" for the change also makes it easier when going to the bank to get change and also makes sure that you will be able to cover the change needed for customers.

The money in the safe should always be counted several times a day. A shift or management change is a good time to do this. This means that any shortages in the money will be found immediately when the audit trail can be traced. The longer the time frame of doubt, then the less likely you will find the problem because too many people will have had a possibility of having caused the shortage.

Making deposits at a bank daily also helps to minimize the possibility of mistakes and theft. The more money that is allowed to accumulate in the safe, the greater the risk. It's also a bigger risk to carry a larger sum of money into a bank.

If a closing manager is responsible for preparing the bank deposit and running reports, then his/her name should be on the bank deposit form with a copy kept. A log of shortages and mistakes should be kept to document who causes a problem. In this way, by looking at the logbook, you will know who needs help in performing their duties as well as who you should be monitoring closely. If you allow a closing manager to make the deposit at the bank, then you need to do so with serious attention to risks involved, not just in mistakes or theft, but also for the safety of the employee and their own personal risks in carrying large sums of cash.

Pulling the cash drawer out of your registers several times a day makes sure that not too much cash will be in a drawer that is opened in front of customers. When customers see a lot of cash, they make the assumption that your business is making a lot of money and they may then think you are overcharging them. Others may think that you are the perfect opportunity to help themselves. You never know who is in your business to just do business and who is there to case the location.

Quick-change artists will usually have a lookout and also know the most vulnerable cashiers to try to trick. A good scam artist can trick a bank teller or a cashier and get up to $200 in a few minutes. They do this by purchasing small items and then starting a series of requests for change, involving larger bills. They try to confuse the cashier by re-counting the change and showing a shortage. They may also physically get loud or pushy and unnerve the cashier. By making a policy that any change, other than just the change given for a purchase can ONLY be done by a manager, these scams can be prevented. Knowing what to look for and shutting the register drawer immediately when a suspected scam artist gets too close should a first line of defense.

Even legitimate customers can be mistaken about what dollar amount they gave you for their purchases. If you always follow stringent cash handling procedures, you will be able to show them correctly what they gave you. When a customer hands you a dollar bill, lay the bill on top of the register drawer far enough away from the customers so that someone couldn't grab it and run, then remove their change, count it out to them and then after the sale is complete, put the dollar bill they gave you into the register drawer. By doing this, at any point that a customer questions what amount they gave you, you have the exact bill right in front of you that they can see. If after the sale is completed and they come back to you and believe they have been short changed, you can be fairly sure that no mistakes were made. If however, there is any doubt, you should be able to run a report on the computerized point of sale system, pull the drawer and count it to determine of there is more in the cash drawer than should be there. This takes time and a patient customer to accomplish this.

We, as a society, are losing basic practical skills. The younger generation is relying more and more on technology to tell them what to do and are not learning abilities such as counting in their head, making and counting change out to a customer or what to do without a calculator or computer. Being able to count out change to a customer without relying on a point of sale system to tell you how much to give back is still a necessary skill. People will always be protective of their money and any business must be competent at handling any situation such as power outages (so that the register cannot tell them what change to give), customers contesting the amount, etc.

⚜ ⚜ ⚜

Let me tell you more...

Sometimes there is just no way to know what human nature will do. I have been amazed at the kindness, consideration and honor some employees have shown. Unfortunately, I have also had some negative experiences with others. Those you think would never be dishonorable or who have had an exemplary record can still do something that stings.

One employee started with me as a seventeen year old. Extremely hard working and smart, he quickly learned every job in the restaurant, was quiet but excellent with fellow employees as well as customers. He was promoted through the ranks so that in five years he was an assistant manager. He started a relationship with one of the other employees whose father came into the restaurant and accused him of poor behavior. Several of us told the man what a hard worker he was and how high his character was. Around this time, we had three customers tell us that they had not received their credit card back after making a purchase in a very busy time and that the next charge (unauthorized) was at a nearby Walmart. We offered to cooperate with authorities and looked at the computer history of our security cameras to see if we could see anything suspicious at our registers. The only person that appeared to be in the vicinity at all three times was this particular assistant manager. Because of his history, no one could believe that he could have anything to do with the credit card fraud and the situation remained a mystery.

Because of the length of time of his service, the assistant manager knew all the computer programs, checks and balances, and ways to beat the system. The catering manager complained one day that someone had voided out one of her orders for over $100. We checked the computer and found an inactive manager code used to void it out, meaning that the money could be removed from a cash drawer even though the customer had paid and no one would know if the catering manager had failed to follow up on her order. A quick audit of the system showed multiple catering orders voided and other large customer orders voided out. It then took several days to go back through available security footage to find out who did the void at a register and this manager was identified as the one who entered the void and removed the cash. It was always at a time when no one else was around that particular register and at off peak times.

Since the employee was under scrutiny and my investigation was ongoing, I made sure he was never allowed to be in the restaurant alone. Finally, he arranged (without permission) to change shifts with others so that he would be the *only* manager on duty an entire Sunday. To his surprise, I showed up at work before him and stayed to close the business too. He had no opportunity to do whatever he had planned. The next day, he called in sick, actually crying on the phone about a death in the family and never showed up for work again so that I could fire him. An audit revealed that he had likely stolen approximately $5000 over six months. All evidence was turned over to police but I allowed them to make the decision whether to pursue it and because I didn't stay on top of them, they eventually dropped it. I'll never know just what triggered the employee to make a choice like that, however, rumors circulated that he had become involved in drugs.

If I had perhaps been more open minded when the girlfriend's father had come in, if I had been more cynical about the manager being the one most likely to be involved with the credit card fraud because of the evidence, perhaps this would have been circumvented, but perhaps not.

⚜ ⚜ ⚜

Secure information.

Profit and loss reporting to the franchisor is a way that the company can determine if your costs are in line with other franchisees and where you are spending your money. This is great if you have an ethical company and can guarantee that your information will remain confidential, but the franchisor will have employees that come and go just like any business. Can you absolutely trust your information is safe from identity theft, other franchisees, talk around the "water cooler" and that business consultants that visit many different franchisees will not disclose anything you don't want disclosed?

If other employees use the computer where you have financial information stored, you need to protect it from unauthorized viewing with passwords. Even if you are satisfied with an employee's performance and trust them, you cannot see the future and know that at some point you may have a falling out. Be wise, and keep this information protected.

All employee files need to be kept in a secure and locked area. Information such as their address, phone number, social security number, job history, performance reviews, etc. is strictly privileged information. Managers may need access to this information, but every manager needs to be warned that the information should never be shared. Also, consider keeping manager files offsite to avoid managers finding out what another manager makes in salary and starting a battle.

Employee Safety.

Keeping your employees safe is not only necessary by law but good business practices because it shows your employees you care. This includes keeping everything in good working order so they can't be hurt, making sure that all cleaning chemicals and anything that could spill or affect their health is always well labeled and kept in a safe place.

Since you have legal issues to deal with here, you must make sure that you understand and adhere to all OSHA safety standards and guidelines. Letting an employee or customer injure themselves or become injured because of negligence can shut down your business. You also need to be overly careful because of those rare people who actually try to find a safety issue and exploit it.

⚜ ⚜ ⚜

Let me tell you more…

Contingency plans are important because you never know when someone will get hurt or a customer may collapse in your business. A manager ended up cutting himself so that he needed stitches and had to leave to go to the clinic. Having a manager leave the premises meant that there would be no one in the building that had the required food safety certification. Also, because of the severity of the cut, he couldn't drive himself so another employee needed to leave to drive him. That meant two people down at a very busy time. We had to hustle to call in another manager and try to get them there quickly. You just can't predict those unfortunate moments.

⚜ ⚜ ⚜

Vendors at your door.

Just because you are paying a vendor, doesn't relieve you from the responsibility to provide a safe environment for anyone performing a service or making a delivery. You need to watch anyone who enters the employee area (particularly) of your business because the vendor's representative can also cause you liability if they sexually harass any employee, slip and fall, damage equipment, or don't provide the exact service that you contracted for.

Representatives that have access to areas where cash is kept, or that get to see your back office operations should be accompanied by an employee at all times.

Many vendors will want to deliver during the night so that they can make their runs more efficient. Most distribution companies work on a model that allows them only so much time to deliver their goods and then get on to the next one. Understandable, but risky if you are the one receiving goods during the night. Anytime your door is open, you are more open to robberies or damage. A delivery person is not going to guard your door while they wheel in a product. Also, exposing your business to a revolving door of different delivery people escalates risk. They will have access to a security code and a key. Often, the franchisor has contracted this and you, as the franchisee, may have no choice. While some businesses never have any problems with this, all it takes is one disgruntled employee or one employee whose background has not been checked extensively enough, for you to become a victim.

In any business, if you have a vendor that provides a service such as cleaning your rugs, they may be accessing areas that show them how you handle your cash or how employees gain access to the building. It is important that you feel comfortable with all the vendors and their representatives.

The ultimate threat, robbery.

When someone with a gun attempts to rob a business, often the person confronting the robber will see only the gun. The police often get a great description of the gun, but not of the robber because guns tend to freeze people in their tracks. Teach your employees not to resist any threat of violence and to do what the robber wants. They should use their observation skills and remember the description so that the robber can be caught afterwards. Everyone should know where the panic alarms are and what procedures to follow if you should be robbed. Review the procedures every six months.

If someone enters the premise and you see that they have a gun under their jacket, let your employees know to watch carefully for suspicious behavior. There are lots of people who now have concealed weapons permits, however, you should never let someone intimidate you or make you afraid.

⚜ ⚜ ⚜

Let me tell you more...

Although we were lucky enough to never suffer a robbery, we did have things disappear. During the height of the copper shortage, one of my managers came to work and set up the restaurant as usual, turning on equipment, starting up the dishwasher, filling the coffee urns, etc. when finally there was no water. She called the water company who came out to find that the water meter had been stolen during the night. We had enough water in the hot water tank and the pipes to do what needed to be done to set up but couldn't run the restaurant until a new meter was put in. Luckily, the shopping center owner had lots of pull with the city and they had it replaced within two hours.

⚜ ⚜ ⚜

Protecting teens.

All machinery that is off limits to teenagers should have a sign posted next to it that anyone under the age of 18 is not allowed to use the equipment. This signals to your employees and customers that you are vigilant, obey the law, and enforce the rules. It will also help with any liability issues if a teenager goes ahead and uses the equipment and gets hurt. With a sign posted, it shows that they disobeyed a policy.

All machinery should always be in good working order and the employees should be taught how to use, maintain and clean any equipment safely. Policies such as unplugging equipment before cleaning should always be enforced. Don't ever walk by an employee using a piece of equipment incorrectly without correcting them because you have just given them "implied" permission to do so.

Look for any possible accidents with electrical cords being too long or getting caught on other things. Observe equipment that might leak or cause burns and look for ways to minimize contact. Let your employees know that safety is a high priority so that they will be careful. Always put out "caution" signs whenever there are safety concerns such as wet floors. You must do everything in your power to protect your employees and customers to alleviate any liability.

Threat of severe weather.

Severe weather should be monitored and a policy in place that will alert employees if the weather is too severe for them to work. This can include snow, tornado alerts, hurricane warnings or severe thunderstorms. Let them know they are expected to show up unless they hear differently. But if things become hazardous while they are on the job, let them know the plan for leaving work so they won't worry and can still perform their job. People love to talk when inclement weather is near and can get caught up in the drama. Employees need to know that they will have plenty of time to leave and get home safely and that you have their best welfare in mind. You may also experience parents not allowing their children to work with just a hint of bad weather.

Employees need to know *how* they will be informed if they should not report for work. They need to know that they should always come to work unless told not to. You need a policy in place to let people know when the business will be closed due to weather extremes and how to get in touch with personnel when the business is closed.

If you lease a building, windows are usually the business owner's responsibility in case of breakage, so beware and make sure your insurance covers them in case of storm damage. In 2004, Southern states experienced multiple hurricanes. After the first one actually hit, everyone boarded up their windows and left town at even a hint of a new hurricane. The cost of lost business was worth more than the possible cost of damage to many of them.

The critical computer backup.

The frequency and amount of computer backup you do is contingent upon how critical your data is. Obviously, the more critical, the more often you need to back up. Some businesses will need to back up every night and others can wait a month. This is one thing that most people neglect and then once a failure occurs, you learn your lesson and back up regularly. It can be exceedingly painful to lose data. Will you lose sales, repair records, profit and loss statements? Recovering lost data, if possible, can take hours and be costly in terms of labor. This should be a scheduled component of your business.

Also, hard copy files need to be protected. Are they close to the floor where a water leak would ruin them? Are they in a locked filing cabinet where a disgruntled employee can do damage to them? Do you keep duplicate copies offsite?

Anyone who has ever had a computer crash without having it backed up will tell you that the time it would have taken them to do the backup in the first place would have been worth its weight in gold. Trying to piece together data can be an overwhelming task. The decision on when to back up is based on just how difficult it would be to recover the data.

Some computer systems allow you to back up your data automatically and it can be backed up onto an external drive or remotely via the Internet in Cloud storage. You must determine what you feel comfortable with. Backing up a computer is not only for possible computer failure but is also insurance in case of floods, fire, theft, etc. All backups should be stored in an offsite location because of this, unless you are using online/Cloud backup.

Safeguarding your computer means restricting access so that employees don't accidentally download a virus, keeping it safe where any environmental issues won't harm it such as keeping cords and power strips off the floor in case a pipe breaks, keeping it in an area of low humidity and normal range of temperature, making sure that nothing can fall on it or spill on it, and then always following your own procedures for backing up the data.

⚜ ⚜ ⚜

Let me tell you more...

That old saying, "when the rat's away, the mice will play" is actually pretty appropriate when you have to leave your business in the hands of immature supervisors or managers that do not see the consequences of their actions. When some of the supervisors were getting bored in the evening and not needed in the main restaurant, they would station themselves in the office and play on the computer. Some of the sites they visited (easily found when looking at the browsing history) were porn or betting sites. They had no idea that they could jeopardize the entire point of sale system or the accounts by accidentally downloading a virus or malware. We acquired a virus once and that was enough to know to check the computer history as often as possible to find out who was viewing what. If they believed they could outsmart me by clearing the history, that was suspicious enough to be called on the carpet.

⚜ ⚜ ⚜

Security systems.
Security systems in your building are essential in today's environment. They help scare away potential burglars when the alarm sounds, they let you know immediately if something has been disrupted and they help protect your investment and your employees. It is important that if you have employees coming and going through a rear entrance during the evening or night that you have a monitor instead the door that shows you who is at the door before it is opened. It is an extra layer of safety against intruders. Sometimes, you see businesses that have propped open their back door either because it is hot inside, someone wants to smoke, or a delivery is being made. This is an invitation for theft. Don't do it.

Leaving work in the dark.
If employees have to park farther away from the building they work in, then nighttime security should be available by adequate lighting or by using a buddy system to walk to their cars. You are responsible for the safety of your employees, especially teenagers. You should always make sure teens are walked to their car by a manager, or they leave in pairs when in the dark or allow them to park closer to the building as an exception. You must also make all reasonable efforts for the safety of all employees so that they do not put themselves in jeopardy because of their job.

Businesses should also make a special effort to keep teens safe, as teens' judgment may not always be to look out for their own safety. Managers should make sure teens get in their car safely and are able to start the car and drive away.

Silent alarms.

Most businesses will have silent alarms by their cash registers and safe. The alarms are generally two buttons that must be pushed at the same time to automatically issue a distress call to the police. These are set up so that the police do not call you to see if it is a false alarm, but immediately dispatch officers to the scene. Although the purpose of having two buttons is so an employee can't accidentally push them together, the curious may still try to do it. Police have policies for false alarms and will charge you money if they come to your business and nothing is wrong.

Camera systems.

In today's Internet world, it is easy to stay connected to your business by cameras. You can watch what is going on in your business in the comfort of your own home. The more cameras you have in your business, the more views you will have at home. This is something that is invaluable. If you ever have a doubt about what an employee is doing on the job when you aren't there, you will know. If you have to trace back any missing money to who took it, it can be done. Cameras will also record a quick-change artist, a customer that deliberately damaged something or stole something as well as show you what happens at night.

⚜ ⚜ ⚜

Let me tell you more...

I had multiple cameras set up in the restaurant with cameras facing all the cash registers, the exits, the kitchen, and the office. Since I also had remote management software set up on the office computer, I could tap into the business computer from my home computer as well as watch the cameras and see who was in the office, all remotely.

My oldest son was a computer whiz and could go into the office computer remotely and fix any prices or make any changes that needed to be done. He could also look at reports or diagnose any issues. One day, he was remotely in the office computer from his apartment at college. He also tapped into the cameras and saw that a manager was in the office. Deciding to play a joke, he wrote on the screen, "What are you doing, Andrew?" and then watched the cameras to see if the manager would notice. It was a priceless moment when the manager saw his name on the screen and while he tried to figure out what was going on. Of course, he knew he could be seen on camera and that we could access the computer remotely so it didn't take to terribly long for him to figure it out, but while he did, it was very funny. It was also a good way to reinforce to employees that you could never tell when the boss would be watching.

⚜ ⚜ ⚜

Employees represent your business.

It is should be common sense to let all employees know that they must act in a safe manor at all times. This can mean that a teenager doesn't try to "lay rubber" when leaving your parking lot or that an employee doesn't get on a ladder wearing flip-flops. Although we want to think that everyone has certain standards, it is important to spell it out.

Using the police.

If anyone notices anything amiss or outside the normal daily routine of the business operations, they should be appreciated or rewarded for coming forward to let you know that something is amiss. For example, if someone walks in wearing a gun holster but you can see it when their coat moves open, then you should know to watch them. They could be part of law enforcement or have a permit but it is wise to beware.

Safekeeping employee and customer records.

You need a safe and secure place to file employee files. Because the files contain sensitive personal information, you must make your best effort to protect them from unauthorized viewing. Managers may need access to the files and anyone doing the hiring, however, they should not be accessible to anyone else. It is best to keep a separate log of employee phone numbers so the employee files are not seen regularly. This protects performance reviews, social security numbers, etc. A locking file cabinet is best so that access is limited.

Other files that may need immediate and unlimited access are the files for equipment. These files should be easily found and contain the instructions for the equipment and recommended maintenance and trouble shooting procedures.

Customer files should also be protected and not readily available. You do not want a disgruntled employee to give information to competitors and you do not want credit information to be seen. Customer files should also be locked.

Other files you may need would be for forms used to run your business: employee applications, policies and procedures, checklists and logs, credit applications, donation requests, etc.

Different ways to organize files include color-coding, file size, labels and placement. Your goal is to make the files that need to be found quickly readily accessible and those files that should be private to be hard to find.

Because of privacy laws, you must be able to prove that you take every measure possible to protect your employee's social security numbers and other private information. Often, a company keeps either a written file or electronic file for an employee. Anyone who has access to the files needs to be controlled and only those with a reason to see the files should be able to see them. Files also contain disciplinary actions and letting other employees see that can have far reaching consequences. Rumors can start or other employees may feel treated unfairly or a host of other problems can surface. You can be held liable for information that is stolen or used to create fake IDs or used for identity theft. You must be able to show, in court if necessary, that you have taken all precautions possible to protect their data.

91

8 Things that Affect Your Choice of Business

Will it provide? How long?

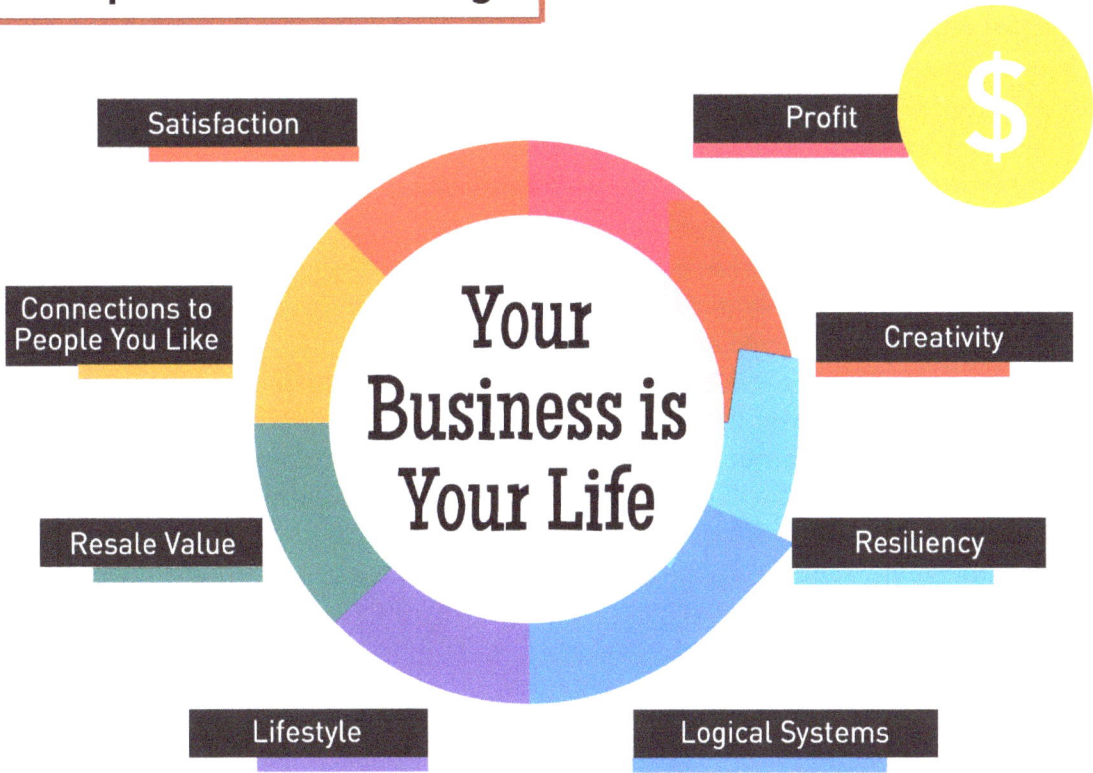

Satisfaction

Profit

$

Connections to People You Like

Your Business is Your Life

Creativity

Resale Value

Resiliency

Lifestyle

Logical Systems

Don't have rose colored glasses on

!

Do your due diligence...research!

YOUR LEGAL REQUIREMENTS

Licenses and permits.

You need to make sure that you adhere to all state, federal and local regulations and that includes having all the licenses that you need to do business. You may need a business license, a restaurant license, etc. There is no way to avoid this and you have to pay a fee. You will have to file an annual report for your business. Ignorance of what you are expected to have is no excuse and you may be cited or prevented from doing business for a while. Do your research and find out what is expected!

In most states, you must file an annual report each year and pay a fee. Generally, the reports just confirm your address and contact information but you must file them on time or risk paying penalties.

Zoning.

One of the most visible ways for people to see what you offer is with the use of neon signs. Many restaurant franchises may require them and they seem to get people's attention. However, there are certain areas where neon signs are not permitted and the farther back your location sits off the road, the less likely it is that people will know you are there without them. Make sure you check the zoning in a potential location BEFORE you decide to lease or build. This little detail can really hurt you. It is also true of regular signage since there may be restrictions on that too.

Even if you believe that you are easily visible from the road, it is amazing to find out just how many people will claim they have never seen your building or can't figure out how to gain entrance. I had a location with signage on two sides of the building, additional signage out in front of the building on a stanchion sign but people still told me they wrestled with finding us.

The building inspector.

If you are involved in a build out of a new or remodeled facility, then a building inspector must approve any construction. Inspections can come into play in other ways too. If you are a restaurant, then the entire blueprints of the design must be approved and depending on the city, can take weeks. Required changes will take longer. That is why it is important to involve someone in the design that is familiar with the city code for restaurants. For example, there are requirements for how many hand sinks need to be in the kitchen or work area. There are rules for the floor drains and signage. There is even an inspection for the dumpster that you will be using and its enclosure. Even if you are ready to open and the shopping center has not met the code for the dumpster, then you will not get to open for business.

⚜ ⚜ ⚜

Let me tell you more...

It was opening day for us and it looked like everything was finally moving along. The health inspector had cleared us and a huge weight had been lifted from me. We opened the doors and were extremely busy taking care of customers. A gentleman wearing a county badge came in and told me that he was a county building inspector and would have to shut us down because the dumpster and it's enclosure had not been cleared and approved as per code. He was very emphatic and said we were violating building codes. I told him that it was owned by the shopping center but he didn't care. I immediately called the landlord and the company's representative came over. The representative took the inspector back to the dumpster enclosure and spent about ten minutes with him there privately. The inspector came back into my restaurant and told me he "forgot" that he already approved the area and then he left, to my great astonishment and also relief. I've always wondered just what went on in those ten minutes.

⚜ ⚜ ⚜

Fire marshal.

The fire marshal will also have to sign off for the plans for your business. You must have enough sprinkler heads per square foot to meet code requirements and many cities require that your building plans go through a different department thus extending the time it takes to get approval. Again, if the city sees anything they don't like then even more time will be taken away. Periodically, a fire marshal will visit your building and if they see anything they don't like such as boxes stacked too close to the ceiling than they can make you change it. They will write a report and then re-visit the premises to make sure you complied with their directives.

⚜ ⚜ ⚜

Let me tell you more...

As with any government policy, it depends on the person doing the job to enforce the codes and how strict they want to be to which determines just how much grief they can cause you. I'm not telling anyone to circumvent the laws but sometimes something will go unnoticed for years and then a new person takes over the inspections and all of a sudden it's a problem. For example, our restaurant had to store lots of items and boxes just after a delivery and those goods had to last a week. We piled things on the shelves so that they wouldn't be in the aisles and so that they would not be a hazard. A new fire marshal walked in and after several years of another fire marshal inspecting our business, the new one determined that we had too much stock too close to the ceilings. He told us that we had to leave an 18" clearance between the boxes and the ceiling tiles. For a business, that's a lot of wasted space. We had no choice but to figure out something else but it was a lot to deal with during a busy period of the day. He also let us know that if he came back and found it the way it was, we would be fined.

⚜ ⚜ ⚜

Health inspector.

If you are a restaurant or a place such as a spa that will require health inspections, then your attitude makes a big difference between an inspector throwing everything at you he can versus being more reasonable. It's important that you view this person as a public servant and a human being and not someone to be adversarial with. Inspectors can write you up for violations, which are published, on the Internet and sometimes in the newspaper. Or, inspectors can pull you aside and give you a heads up off the record about something he/she wants you to change or do differently. Making sure the inspector is respected and listened to makes a much better working relationship. They can show up during a busy time, they can show up more often and they can make your life miserable.

We always made sure that the inspector was accompanied by a manager who took notes of everything the inspector said. That shows an attitude of trying to do everything correctly. What is one inspector's irritation may not bother another. For example, we served sliced lemons in a dish with ice under it next to the iced tea urn. After about four years, a new inspector came along and insisted that the lemons be covered. With customers constantly uncovering the lemons, they were still often uncovered. A health inspector who wanted to be insistent could have seen that as a continued violation and subtracted points from the future inspections. That could lead to a totally different solution for serving lemons.

Sales tax filing.

Sales tax is usually monitored and collected by the state. You must file with them for a special identification number and then you must file reports at the end of each month or quarterly as per their requirements. In my state, if you do not owe anything since you didn't sell anything that required tax, you *STILL* have to file a report for zero dollars. The failure to do so results in a fine, no matter what. They will often give you one warning before they charge you but you need to be aware that reports must be done on time, once you have an identification number. One business I heard about had no sales for months, however, since they failed to file their report that actually owed several hundred dollars in fines.

Generally, you do not have to collect sales tax from non-profit organizations but you do need to get a copy their exemption certificate and keep it on file. You don't collect sales tax on items that are sold to someone else as "wholesale" when they will collect sales tax from the end consumer or for raw materials that will be used to create an end product that is sold to a consumer. If you sell over the Internet, you must collect sales tax if you have a physical presence in the state to which you are selling. This means a rented, leased or owned building. These laws are changing as the Internet becomes a bigger influence, so always check for the latest legal requirements.

Many counties collect sales tax. You must make sure that whoever programs your point of sale system, uses the correct percentage. It can be tragic to find out you have only been collecting 1% for them when it should have been 2%. Once found, it is up to you to pay the difference.

Doing Business As (DBA).

In many cases, you will want to use a different name for your actual business (the one the state knows) rather than the one you do business as (DBA) to the public. In cases of franchises where there may be hundreds of units all calling themselves by the same name, you must file this name called a *fictitious name* with the state. For example, if XYZ Restaurants have 200 units, all of them have a fictitious name of XYZ Restaurant and the actual business name is the name that the individual owner named their business. So if, Dan Smith named his business Dan Smith Enterprises and owned a XYZ Restaurant franchise, he would say he is Dan Smith Enterprises DBA (doing business as) XYZ Restaurant.

This can be confusing to vendors sometimes if they service multiple franchise units, which are owned by many different owners. The only way to differentiate the units is by their address and often one unit may receive an invoice belonging to another owner.

Filing documents with the government for employees.

You must adhere to all legal requirements for filing that you have hired an employee. You must use legal documents that show valid social security numbers and other forms of identification. You are signing the forms testifying to the fact that what you saw was accurate and legal. These forms will be used to withhold taxes and also for forwarding of final paychecks if the employee leaves.

Keeping abreast of health permits.

If you are a restaurant or anything that requires a health permit such as a spa, you must submit forms to the local government to apply to be this type of vendor and will submit your building design to the permitting department for review before you will be allowed to build or finish out a space.

If you handle food, you must comply with all laws that state how many managers must be on hand every minute that have food safety training at a management level and that each employee has the lower level of food safety education. In my state, a management level food safety employee must be on site at all times to monitoring actions and each employee must have undergone the condensed version of this training. Health inspectors will check your files to make sure everyone is up to date.

Closing out the business.

In the legal business world, it is important that if you close your business, or if you change the way you do business, you actually close accounts that you have for vendors. This helps assure that they vendor won't come back four years later and tell you that there is an unpaid invoice. States have different statutes of limitations on the time that you will still be liable for an open invoice, but you need to protect yourself and keep accurate records of dates closed and whom you spoke with. This is especially true of state and local county and city requirements. If you close your business, you also must close your company with all state and local governments.

Your Success FORMULAS

Starting a business may sound impossible to many, but if you have the right skills and are willing to do some hard work, it can be profitable and fulfilling.

The Profit Formula

Profit = Sales - (Product Cost + Labor Cost) - (Fixed + Variable Costs)

Example:
Sales = $1,700,000
Product Cost (your cost to purchase the products) = $612,000
Labor Cost (wages + payroll taxes) = $540,000
Fixed and Variable Costs (rent, utilities, insurance, taxes, etc.) = $429,000
Net Profit = $1,700,000 - $612,000 - $540,000 - $429,000
Net Profit = $119,000 (7%)

01

Cash Flow = Profit (from above) + Depreciation

Example:
Depreciation = $10,900
Cash Flow = $119,000 + 10,900
Cash Flow = $129,900

The Value Formula (Profitability Index)

Profitability Index must be equal or greater than 1 to move forward!

Profitability Index = Present Value of Future Cash Flow ÷ Initial Investment

02

Example:
Cash flow from above = $129,000
Assume a 10 year term for the business
Present Value = 10 X $129,000 = $1,290,000
Initial Investment = $1,000,000
$1,290,000 ÷ $1,000,000 = 1.29 (Good!)

OPERATIONS

Getting prepared to open.

If you are a restaurant, then there are a lot of things that have to happen before you can open and every hour that you delay your opening is money flowing out the window. You must hire and then train all your employees. The time spent in training is crucial but you need to bring in money to cover their wages so you need to open as soon as possible. If you are a restaurant or by law need a health inspection, the health inspector must come and sign off on your facility and procedures before you can open your door to paying customers. In some states, you are allowed to GIVE your food away for free if you have not had your health inspection. This is good if you have not been able to get your inspection but you have already published your opening date. That's costly, but must be weighed against having customers show up and finding out that you aren't open. They may never come back.

To kick start your business, invitations are usually handed out for a "friends and family" event where food is given away for free but gives your employees a chance to practice with a real crowd. Then, you may want to invite businesses and their employees to come for free food too. Some franchises will require this.

If you are another type of business, you will still have to make sure that you have met all legal requirements (licenses, building inspections, etc.) before you can open and still must train your employees. All the time spent in waiting costs you money.

⚜ ⚜ ⚜

Let me tell you more...

Since we did not know when we would get our health inspection and had difficulty getting a response about when it would be, we had to rely on last minute invitations given out to local businesses. On the morning of our health inspection, we visited local businesses with written invitations inviting all their employees to come dine for free. Opening at 11:30 was one of the most stressful days ever, not knowing if anyone would show up. However, at 11:30, cars began to roll into the parking lot until the restaurant was overflowing with people. The offer of free food was enough to get everyone to come try us out.

⚜ ⚜ ⚜

Forecasting.

Forecasting your sales and production accurately is critical to your business for cost control and profit potential. If your business is new and you have no history to base your estimates on than you have to forecast upwards for sales to make sure you have enough product to sell. Not having enough product would be disastrous for a new business. A possible way to get an estimate for your sales is to ask the franchise company for their estimates based on what other franchisees have done their first year. You can get a feel for how long it takes to actually make a profit, how many employees you need to hire when you open (you need to figure on hiring extra employees to get the right people to stay with you for the long term), the opening product order, the amount of customers you can expect for your opening and a host of other information. Look at the competition, look at the economy and then you must make some educated judgments.

Your POS computer system will accumulate information and give you reports that can tell you how much you did in sales by category, by day, by month, etc. You just have to be in business long enough to have a history. This information will serve you well in the future.

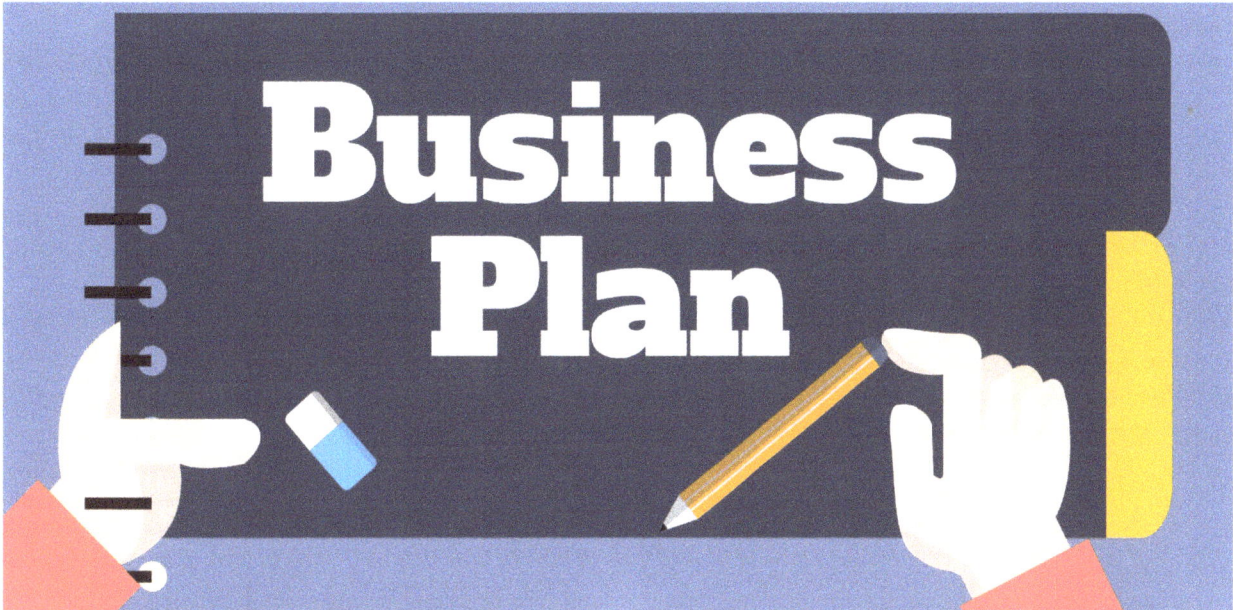

Business Plan

Executive Summary

Vision, Mission, Values

Plan Elements

Site selection
Employees
Management
Pricing
Operations
Training
Profitability
Vendors/Suppliers

Location/Building

Interior Design

store

Shopping Center Design

Demographics

Surrounding population
Household income
Number of cars passing by
Projected growth
Number of families
Number of households
Number of businesses near

Insurance for your business.

Insurance costs can be a surprise. You must make sure you are covered for Fire/Hazard, Liability, Medical, and Workers Compensation Insurance. Additionally, whoever finances your business may require that you personally be covered by life insurance so that if you die, the financial obligation is still paid back. You may also want to maintain an umbrella policy personally so that if someone sues your business, you can protect your personal assets. Just because you have set up your business to make sure you are protected on a personal level doesn't mean you *will* be in every situation.

Having *loss of business insurance* gives you some additional peace of mind. If you have a catastrophe such as a weather event and have your roof blown off, you would be able to receive an amount from the insurance company equivalent to what would normally be brought in by sales, as well as the amount of the damages.

⚜ ⚜ ⚜

Let me tell you more...

It takes months and months sometimes to get a franchise open. It can be delayed because of design issues, permitting or a multitude of things. I signed by lease one year in the summer and finally got opened by May the following year. Just in that time frame, several insurance companies stopped doing business in my state and the ones that remained increased their rates dramatically. Instead of paying what I had for my first location, the second location cost me $7000 more per year, an entirely unplanned for cost.

My franchisor required that we have patio seating with outdoor furniture and patio umbrellas. The area was very popular and since it seated a lot of people would be crowded on weekends where bike riders would stop for coffee or people with dogs would sit.

The umbrellas were inserted into a heavy metal stand with a knob that turned to tighten them down. At night, they were removed and carried inside. At times the wind would pick up and damage some of the umbrellas and at other times the wind would whip up so quickly that there was barely enough time to notice the patio and run outside to collapse the umbrellas. If they weren't collapsed during windy episodes they may cause the tables to turn over or the metal rails underneath the umbrella to bend.

Twice, employees failed to tighten the knob during windy days and the umbrellas took off on their own, sailing through the air to land on a customer's car in the parking lot. Once it landed on a Cadillac convertible (with its top up) and ripped a hole in the roof's fabric. Another time the top of the umbrella scraped a car's side. Insurance paid for it but it was an unnecessary expense. If the umbrellas had been tightened down correctly, we may have suffered damage, the customer would not have.

⚜ ⚜ ⚜

The business consultant.

The business consultant that is assigned by the franchisor to help you with your opening and keeps in contact with you throughout your years in business, may also be the one responsible for performing inspections of your franchise. If so, they must walk a fine line between doing their job for the franchisor and inspiring, motivating and educating you and your employees. The best business consultant knows when to let the little stuff go and focus on the issues that will bring more profit to both you and the franchisor. If they have an adversarial relationship with you, no one wins.

Having had several different business consultants during my time as a franchisee, I can say that they are as different as anyone's personality is different. One lived their life for the company, eating and breathing the philosophy. Another had some ego issues and made sure to always find at least something out of order just so he could tell you what you were doing wrong. Another was more of a buddy, the kind of person that if you were nice to, wouldn't hurt you in the inspection. He was just marking time, not really into his job. Who did I learn the most from? The first one who loved his job. Who did I enjoy hosting the most? The third one who made it easy to talk to and actually addressed issues in a down to earth way.

Here is an actual account from a business consultant who performed inspections in a different industry, but still a retail oriented business. You can see what he noticed and what affected him the most when doing an audit.

⚜ ⚜ ⚜

Let a corporate business consultant tell you more...

"The auditing work that I was involved with at 'XYZ Company' came on the heels of a new inventory process/system that was sorely needed in the company. Prior to this initiative, the company would roll out new processes from time to time and the stores would basically blow them off given the lack of enforcement and follow through at the corporate level. This attitude on corporate initiatives filtered down with the results being project failure. New blood was brought in at the corporate level with new ideas and processes and they were dedicated to making them work.

The new inventory process was introduced to all the stores, and store management was clearly informed that this was *serious*. They were going to be held accountable for following the given instructions and the new process. It was about three or four weeks into this new initiative that I got a phone call informing me that I was going to be involved in the initial follow up "surprise" audits of the stores to check for compliance. I was given a checklist, a list of stores, and instructions to keep my scheduled store visits confidential to make this as honest as possible.

The stores were responsible for maintaining three systems of data (requirements that were provided by the corporate offices). It had to do with checking stocked inventory on the shelves, and "shooting" the UPC labels (with a handheld device) of items that were out of stock, then they had to verify on the computer system to confirm that they were truly out of stock on that item, etc. My checklist involved checking the systems to make certain the stores were complying with the process, doing spot checks for accuracy, and walking the store aisles for a look/see in general.

To demonstrate the store attitude that existed before this "getting serious" business, I remember at the very first store I visited, I asked the store manager to see his three systems of information and he literally laughed in my face and said, "We're not doing that shit." The information was nowhere to be found. My responsibilities in the audit process were to report my findings to the corporate office.

Anyway, as an auditor and having a field job, I was a representative of the corporate office. There would be some individuals in that position that would let the power go to their head. I wasn't like that. My job was to check compliance, point out the areas of non-compliance, remind the stores how to comply and make sure they understood the process, and report my findings. I didn't act like a corporate "big wig" or anything like that. I always tried to be very respectful as if I was walking into someone's 'house.' But the respect should work both ways. For example, yes, the manager that laughed in my face didn't make me happy in the least. I still completed the audit, reported my findings, etc. But I could have not been more disrespected. There are plenty of other auditors that would find everything they could to black mark a store given that situation. I didn't believe in doing that, but I very well may be in the minority.

I walked into a store to conduct an audit and there was one of the managers lying on the floor in the doorway of the manager's office eating her lunch (located immediately in front of the cashier lines.) Here I did play the 'corporate card' and told the woman who I was and that I was from the corporate office. She still sat on the floor eating her lunch, unaffected by what I just told her. I didn't hold this against the store in the audit process, but you can be sure that I reported the incident to the corporate office. Lying on the floor eating lunch, not caring that a corporate representative was visiting, and all this playing out in front of customers!

I would say that the best advice to give a store that is being audited for compliance is to show respect, and to expect it as well. The best stores that I visited may not have had the best scores, but they were ones where at least two managers followed me around as I walked about the store, taking notes, and asking questions on things they may have been unsure of. They didn't do this to stroke my ego, but it was because they cared enough to do better....respect! Not just respect for me, but for the company and themselves.

When things did not go well from a personality or respect standpoint, I didn't intentionally look for things to 'ding' the store on, but there are plenty of auditors that would. Actually, if I felt the respect was there and that there was a somewhat honest effort being made, I let some things slide in some of the gray areas. I just asked them to do a better job with it.

As an auditor, what I didn't like to hear was a bunch of excuses. I audited one particular store that scored very low. In my conversation with the female store manager afterward, she broke down and cried, telling me how hard she was trying and that she was scared to lose her job, etc. They were all just excuses as it was obvious to me that the effort was not being made. In this case I made sure that I personally contacted the corporate office by phone, telling him the result and how absolutely distraught that she was about it.

I think a good auditor should not only check compliance, but also provide good guidance for stores that have strayed off the path. But stores can't anticipate and sadly should not expect that from the auditor. The best action they can take is to be respectful, to acknowledge any criticism not with excuses, but perhaps soliciting suggestions on what they can do to make things better (if the situation is appropriate.) An auditor will always keep an eye and an ear open for anything going on in the store that may not be on a checklist, such as a customer complaining and that the manager doesn't address them properly, a customer complaining about a product, wet floors, unsafe conditions, etc.

Whatever the auditor ego situation, an auditor doesn't want to be ignored. They have an important job to do and they do not want to be blown off (respect again!) But if a customer is complaining and/or there is an urgent matter to be taken care of, it is not only appropriate for the manager to excuse themselves from the auditor; it is paramount that they do so.

Ultimately, regardless of personalities and egos of auditors and store managers/owners alike, the store should recognize that the auditor's purpose is in the best interest of the company. The store should be respectful, provide all information the auditor requests without hesitation, and not make excuses if they are found to be non-compliant in certain areas. However difficult it may to accept, the store should recognize non-compliance as a challenge for improvement."

⚜ ⚜ ⚜

You may end up having the same business consultant for years so it behooves you to maintain a good relationship with him/her. They can do you a lot of damage and they can be a lot of help. The way you treat them will have a considerable effect since they are just human. Many consultants go through the company's training program just as you or your managers did, so do they always know better than you? No, but they also have a direct channel to people that can help you so it's still a good idea to have that positive relationship.

In my experience, having a good relationship usually meant getting a "heads up" that an inspection was due. They would leak little tidbits of information to let you know the kinds of things that the franchisor had directed them to be particularly picky about. Having a week or two to do an extra bit of deep cleaning, or organizing your back office was quite nice.

Labor cost and scheduling.

Scheduling your labor is one of the most valued skills of owning a business and one of the most critical components of profit and loss. The goal is to schedule your employees so that it is the most cost efficient while still maintaining excellent customer service. Too much labor and your profit is eaten up, not enough labor and you lose customers and sales. Making sure there is a smooth transition between shifts is necessary but too much overlap can really eat up the payroll hours (and profit).

You must also find the right mix in the employee pool of skill, availability (including transportation and their lifestyle), what you pay them, and how they benefit your business. For example, some people will only work for you if they get a full forty hours a week, some people want part time and some people will have restricted hours because this will be a second job for them. If you are a business whose sales are seasonal, or are tied into the economy or have odd hours, keeping employees can be a challenge even in a poor economy when people need jobs.

The cost for labor varies widely from state to state and within geographic areas. It depends on the mix of people and the cost of living. If you're looking for minimum wage labor but your business is in a very affluent area, you may have trouble pulling in enough candidates if there is not adequate public transportation. Conversely, if you need skilled labor, or highly educated employees, will you be able to entice them to come to your area if you are in a lower income district?

Each period that you schedule for (assume you schedule one week in advance) would involve a spreadsheet of labor with all the hours listed of each day that you are open. You input the name of the employee and their pay rate and then follow through each day of the week and input their shift hours (actual times working). The total column will show what your labor cost for the week is per employee (don't forget to add in payroll taxes). If you know that you are heading into a downtime for your business then you can see where each employee is scheduled and figure out where you need to cut costs. By cutting off fifteen minutes here or there of an employee's shift, you may arrive at a labor cost you can live with.

Not only must you be aware of labor costs each hour and day, you must be aware of what positions an employee can handle. If one employee is trained to handle multiple positions or jobs, he is more valuable because he can step in when another employee calls off sick or fill in for fifteen minutes until a new employee arrives. You must also be aware of minors working and the breaks they must take and make sure that another employee can handle the minor's tasks while the minor is taking the required break.

Working with an employee's requests for certain hours can take you more time when doing the schedule but usually pays off in loyalty. Most employees really appreciate an employer listening to their needs for time with their family or even for working second jobs. The more flexible you can be, the more the employee will be likely to stay with you, even if they don't make as much money as with someone that would give them NO input.

There are many labor scheduling programs available and some are bundled with the POS system. You should estimate your sales each day and divide it into segments (equivalent to job shifts or by the hour) and then it will show you how much you can spend on labor. You use a formula as a goal such as targeting 30% of your sales as a labor cost. Then, by actually putting together a job schedule based on the actual employee wages, you can see how far off your target you are and make changes accordingly.

Sometimes a business will have to save labor costs at nonpeak times so they are well covered during busy times. However, this means taking the risk that you may become busy during the slower time when you don't have the optimal employee coverage and thus alienate customers.

Once a business has been open for some time and gone through all the seasons of a full year, the labor scheduling is much more accurate because you have an actual history of sales to work with. You will know what happens in snowy or rainy weather, if your customers still arrive or if they stay at home.

How to train anybody.

Everybody learns differently. Some people learn by watching or being shown pictures of what to do. Some people learn by listening to someone tell them what to do. Some people must experience the task themselves to learn it. Your trick is to figure out the quickest and shortest way to teach someone a new task and get them up and running in their job in the shortest amount of time. This may take some experimentation or an all around approach. For example, you may let an employee watch a "how to" video, then quiz them about what they saw, and then ask them to perform the task. This hits all the major areas of learning and hopefully, the employee will absorb the knowledge.

⚜ ⚜ ⚜

Let me tell you more...

When you have a lot of employees or there is quite a bit of turnover, a fun and creative way to train employees was to let everyone take part in a training video, which was edited to show an overview of the restaurant and its positions. We used a camcorder, some video editing software and then added music and voiceovers to create a fifteen-minute video that a new employee could watch by themselves. The video gave an overview of our company culture, showed the different people engaged in doing their job and explained a bit about them and their job descriptions. We used fun music and even added in bloopers.

⚜ ⚜ ⚜

Motivation.

Motivating employees is a science itself. Everyone is motivated by a slightly different mix of things. Some employees will want to engage in social activities with other employees and some will want to just do their job and go home. As an owner, it is your challenge to find a way to motivate each employee in the way he/she needs to be motivated.

As people get older, they usually become motivated more by money than other perks. They don't feel the need for recognition as much, nor want to know that they you approve of them. Usually the younger a person is, the more they need to gain positive feedback, be recognized for a job well done or see an upward career path. Older employees may be more concerned with security and a way to save for retirement.

Generally, people need to know what is expected of them and then a mixture of performance based rewards or bonuses helps to encourage superior efforts. However, some people may see such goals as too lofty and not be motivated by them. You might consider doing some type of random rewards such as giving someone a gift card when they make a particularly difficult customer happy or when they show up early and are ready to work on the dot. That kind of randomness encourages people to do good deeds throughout their day.

Of course, managers need to set good examples by maintaining a positive attitude; nothing can bring down your employees more than a manager who doesn't appreciate those who work for him/her or complains themselves. Managers need to set the tone of the business by showing a good face, keeping negative comments to themselves and knowing when to compliment the employee. Managers can be game changers and one who the employee really enjoys working for is invaluable to an owner. If the employees see the manager as too narrow minded, lazy or dumb, you will have a morale problem. If the manager is respected and admired then the employees will be more likely to give their best effort.

Anything you set up to help motivate employees must be good for you and good for the employees. If you decide that you want to set a reward as a company trip to the beach and your employees don't want to travel or leave their families behind, then it is not a motivator. A universal reward is always money, however, that can get boring so if you mix it up with gift cards, dinners, shopping sprees or an extra paid day off, then you still continue to motivate the majority of your staff.

Some of examples of motivation programs include:
1. Profit Sharing
2. Employee of the Month
3. Contests with awards, privileges or prizes
4. Awards for attendance
5. Bonuses for excellent performance

Any program that you create needs to be easily understood, the rules clear and the award or prize spelled out. Too many details left out can lead to hurt feelings and misunderstandings. The award should be attainable but not too easily so and should be given immediately to a winner.

If you want to offer profit sharing as an incentive, as a small business, you would then have to reveal your financials or have a way to prove to the employee that what they are getting is accurate. Mistrust can be an ugly creature to tamp down if employees feel you are holding back on them after being promised something. Employees also have to have a way to influence the outcome so that their hard work can actually make more money. If they can't, then the incentive is pointless anyway. For example, if you give out a percentage of the profits and your profits are directly related to how many customers you have in any one month, then if you don't advertise or do your part to bring new customers in, there is not much that an employee can do to affect the profit.

I found that in my restaurant an employee of the month who received a $50 bill for being voted the best by the other employees worked well for a limited time. For the first several months, truly the best and hardest working received the vote, but after a while it appeared that everyone had gotten together and decided to just rotate who got the money and it no longer was a reward for hard work, but more about who everyone liked. That meant it was time to change the reward system.

Of course, everyone needs money to live on but some employees will be earning money to support a family and other employees will only need to support themselves. Some will need money to finance a hobby and some will spend every part of their paycheck each week.

⚜ ⚜ ⚜

Let me tell you more...

As with any job that is highly repetitive, it takes a lot to keep employees excited and engaged with their job so that each and every customer experiences the best service. One way to amp up the enthusiasm is to have employee contests, employee rewards and employee of the month programs.

To integrate learning and reinforcement into the job, we often played a type of "poker" where employees had to answer a question about a function of their job, the product or the restaurant. If they answered correctly, they got to pick a card out of a deck. They held onto the card until all the employees had the chance to earn the same number. Then the cards were revealed to find the best hand of cards, according to poker rules. The winner earned ten dollars, but the excitement the game generated went a long way.

Other games were contests to create new products out of a few ingredients presented. Although by franchise agreement, we couldn't offer the products for sale, everyone had fun in trying to be creative and win a small prize. Sometimes, we had coffee drink contests, having the employees create something unique and then had a panel of customers judge the new product and vote on the best idea. It created lots of excitement, fun and teamwork. Especially the younger employees enjoyed the creative atmosphere and were very enthused.

⚜ ⚜ ⚜

Motivate Your Employees

Profit Sharing

You must share your financials to prove employees are getting their fair share.

Employee of the Month

Recognition and a small prize shows appreciation.

Contests

Awards, privileges or prizes add excitement.

Attendance Awards

You show that you acknowledge effort.

Bonuses

Bonuses can be unexpected or tied to specific goals.

Good communication.

Good, clear communication is so important to a business that everyone should understand the modes and means of effective communication. Verbal communication, while using the voice, also entails body language, eye contact, the emotions and intellect, and an exchange of energy. Often people pick up a feeling from another, even though they are saying something else. Don't discount this. Communication should flow from the top down in the organization, from the bottom up and side to side among peers. A person's background, his/her education level, their heritage and customs all affect the attitude they take when communicating with others. As a business owner, you cannot afford to let anyone say anything that offends another person, as there is liability involved. Poor communication leads to errors and mistakes. Good communication leads to an efficient, effective business model.

Everyone has played the "telephone" game where a person whispers a sentence to another person and then that person whispers to another and so forth until you finally get through 10-15 people and what is being spoken bears no resemblance to the original sentence. Any communication that is allowed to travel from person to person risks being inaccurate. Important communication should be given directly to a person *in* person or in writing. All written materials should be grammatically correct with proper spelling. When things are misspelled people tend to discount the content.

Psychologists say that communication is 7% what is said, 38% how it is said and 55% facial and body language. So just instructing an employee how to say something doesn't necessarily work for everyone. The employee must be aware of all facets of communication. Employees at all levels and across the board must practice good strong levels of communication with one another and with vendors and customers as well.

The old saying that first impressions are worth a thousand words means that before even a word is said, the observer is looking over the person and forming opinions based on a number of items. Things such as hygiene, grooming, the manner of dress be it casual or professional, the colors being worn, posture, eye contact, body language (do they slouch or cross their arms?), hair color and style, an air of confidence or failure, clothes that are new or well worn, even down to whether their shoes are clean are all absorbed by the observer in an instant. Once the person speaks, even more levels of analysis take place and more judgments are formed. So, if there is a way to level the playing field so that all judgments come back as "professional" then there is less room for misunderstandings and error.

Written communication should also always be professional. Because it can be used as proof that someone said something, writing anything down becomes a testimony to the person who is the author: how well they said something, how diplomatic it was and what the tone was. Never write when angry or frustrated.

In a business situation, when dealing with so many different personalities, backgrounds and expectations, it is always wisest to say things to employees in the most concise way possible. For example, an owner could tell an employee to "go clean out the storage area". A better way to say it would be to "ask" the employee to "would you go clean out the storage area, please." You shouldn't have to give orders because the fact that you are the boss should be enough. If you do, then you have other issues.

You could also make your request even clearer by saying that your goal was to clear off at least two shelves or that you wanted a clear pathway to an item and proceed to explain what could be condensed or thrown away or relocated.

Every employee should be instructed how to speak and write in a professional manner as soon as they are hired. This means instruction on not using words in the work place such as curse words or slang, understanding what sexual harassment entails including words, pictures or anything that might offend someone, not using labels for people or ethnic backgrounds and not carrying jokes too far so that they insult another employee. You never know who might overhear what is said. Even if an employee is speaking another language, a customer just might understand it.

Starting a conversation with anyone, especially someone you don't know well, can be easy if you establish some type of rapport first. This means that you relate to the other person in a way that shows you are creating a connection. You might give them a sincere compliment, you might comment or ask about their day off or comment on the job they are doing. Being friendly in this way can put another at ease and start a good rapport. Look for things you have in common and start there.

When you need to communicate, set a goal so that you will know if you met your expectation after the communication is over. Be sure to keep it simple, so that you will know if you are successful or not. Your goal could be as simple as gaining agreement as to a meeting place for lunch. The more you learn to set goals, the more your communication will evolve and become second nature. By seeing results you will know if you have really communicated with the other person.

Anytime you try to engage another in communication means it flows back and forth so when one speaks, the other listens. Many of us don't really listen anymore and are already thinking of the next thing we will say when we should be listening to the speaker. A sign of a good listener is that they will paraphrase what they just heard and say it back to the speaker in a slightly different manner to show they understood. For example, the speaker would say that they are finished with a project and ready to take a break. The listener might paraphrase that and say, "So what you're telling me is that after your break you are ready to turn in your results and start a new project?" Then the speaker can respond and clarify the communication. Paraphrasing also shows the speaker that you really did listen and understand them. You should be careful not to sound condescending, however.

If you are trying to teach someone something, be aware that each individual learns in different ways: some people learn by seeing it written or drawn on paper, others learn by hearing about it, and others learn by trying it in a *hands on* approach. So, if you find that you are not getting through to someone in one way, try another way until the person can show or tell you what he or she has learned. Having some type of test shows you how effectively you trained your employee. It can be written, verbal, or hands on.

Poor communication can be a source of problems that tend to compound themselves the longer the issue lasts. Take for example the issue of an employee not feeling recognized for a job well done. The more they stew about it, the angrier they become and it then affects their future performance. However, an employee that gets an immediate and appropriate "pat on the back" feels motivated to continue their hard work.

A workplace that does not dispel gossip creates an atmosphere of "misinformation" that builds on itself to damage relationships and the line of command. Sometimes, the lack of communication can cause people to make assumptions that may or may not be accurate and then take actions based on those assumptions. Perhaps an event happens and no information is passed along to clarify what happened, then people will start to make assumptions based on their own past experiences and base of knowledge. Perhaps a franchisor sends in a business consultant to inspect your location and the employees see the owner and the consultant in a heated discussion. The two may have been discussing their favorite team's basketball scores but the perception of the employees may be that there are problems brewing between the two. Although a business owner doesn't need to share every facet of their business with their employees, being observant will let you know when employees need to know more.

Every person at a company will have come from a different background, have different education levels, different goals and different expectations about the workplace. Some people work to live their life in a certain style while others have a strong work ethic and want to do their best no matter what. Any type of communication has to take into account that each person is different and attempt to get through to all types of personalities, ages, genders and socioeconomic groups.

If you are communicating in a one-on-one situation, relating more specifically to the individual and their differences will be appreciated. If you have a bilingual employee that speaks Spanish and you make an effort to greet them in their native language, you instantly show respect for them as an individual. Knowing that someone has a son that has just won a scholarship to college and remarking on that before any communication takes place shows the employee that you recognize them as an individual and that you remember who they are and care about them.

Dealing with an employee that is upset should be a priority. Make sure that if an employee is visibly upset, they are given the opportunity to compose themselves before a discussion takes place. It should also take place privately (unless this would cause greater upset or legal liabilities) and the employee should be dealt with compassionately. Even if the employee is mistaken about whatever made them upset, you can always say sincerely that you are sorry they are upset without taking blame for the situation or accepting responsibility for it. Allow the employee to say their mind and listen first, then reply. In any situation where an employee has accused someone of doing something to them that will cause you or your business financial or legal harm, always follow the letter of the law and procedures for investigating the allegations and following through with a solution. Remember though, accusations of sexual harassment or harassment of any kind call for swift and thorough solutions to the problem.

Any time that something is very important, make sure the communication is more than just verbal. If it involves an issue where an employee could be fired if they don't obey a new rule, then put it in writing, post it on a bulletin board and then make every employee sign the new rule on a separate sheet of paper and file it in their employee file. This covers you legally as well as confirms that they truly understand the importance of the new rule. Have a meeting, work one on one or make a video that the employees watch to explain it.

Show employees good examples of communication by doing role-plays in meetings. Pretend to be disgruntled customers, co-workers having a disagreement, or even a distracted manager with a problem at home. Show the employees what to say and how to say it to get the other person to listen and not take offense. Make policies and stick to them about using clean language, not making offensive jokes or talking about others behind their backs.

Unfortunately, customers are NOT always right, however, they always have to be treated with respect and with an appreciation for their business. Your employees need to learn to deal with an upset customer and when to pass the customer off to a manager with greater authority to fix the problem. You must also protect your employees from an abusive customer and know when to recommend to the customer that he does not come back.

Not only do employees need to understand how to communicate but *when* to communicate. They will not have the same perspective as an owner because it is not their assets at risk or their reputation. However, they can understand that what affects the owner will eventually affect them by trickling down. So, they should be made to understand that if they stand by and see something happen that is suspicious or a cause for concern and not report it, it is a violation of policy.

Employees should know that if they think something is not as it should be, they should tell a manager.

Everyone involved in the business should pick the right time to communicate. When customers are being taken care of, when managers are counting money or when a manager has a lunch break, it is a wise employee who chooses the correct time to ask questions or start a conversation so that they do not interrupt. An owner should not automatically assume that all employees are at the same level in their judgment but may have to set standards, issue policies and educate the employees and managers.

An employee should understand the organization chart. If they have a training question, whom should they approach? If they have a policy question, where do they find the answer? If they have a complaint, who will listen and take action? If they need a day off or extra help, what person will give them the honest and correct answer? Make sure that you know your own organization and be clear and who reports to whom, and who has authority over whom even if you are a small business.

Manager log.

When you have a business where the shifts do not overlap (or even if you do), it becomes crucial that you have a method of communicating what happened during the previous shifts. For example, if you had a run on a certain type of product in the evening and that's why the opening manager the next day can't find any left, then it needs to be communicated so the opening manager doesn't go crazy searching for it. We created a "manager log" where each manager in every shift had to write at least a sentence about what happened during their day. It could be as little as "good day, everything smooth" or it could say, "little girl lost her bracelet, be on the lookout" or it could say, "got complaints about the ham, we need to check the rest of the shipment." It especially gave a "heads up" for any issues or problems to look out for.

A short paragraph of anything that happened during their shift will alert a manager just coming in if there were any maintenance issues, that an employee called in sick, if there is a special order, if a customer was dissatisfied, that a piece of equipment broke, or anything else of importance. This should be a required policy in a business where managers may not always see one another face to face. The manager log is also very beneficial when trying to go back and find out when a piece of equipment broke or when a repairman promised to show up. You have a record of events as they occur and you never know when you will need to follow up on a critical piece of information. If the closing manager found anything off for the day in the money or if they had a problem with an employee, this would be the place to write it down. If the issue were really critical, then they would be expected to call too, and let everyone know.

We divided the pages of the log into sections on each day, which were titled: Equipment, Employees, Operations and Sales. We would also write on the next day if something were supposed to happen. Knowing that a maintenance man is scheduled to show up in the afternoon means the manager will follow up if the maintenance man doesn't appear. Knowing that they will be short handed because an employee is at the doctor will enable the manager to schedule his own workload better. Seeing that sales were up means the manager needs to gear up to be busy. All those "heads up" situations can help the manager coming on duty to function better.

The longer you are in business, the more you will realize that you must write just about everything down to be able to document it for all sorts of reasons. Trying to remember that day when the soccer tournament came to town in the spring and the restaurant was slammed? Refer back to the manager log.

Sample Manager Log

Date: April 29, XXXX

Catering:
Delivery scheduled for 3pm. Set up bags prepared and on shelf. Invoice complete. Susan will deliver. Set aside an extra dozen chocolate chip cookies.

Shift Summary:
Crazy day. Did $6000 in sales. Very short staffed, very busy. Got slammed with a line to the door from 4 pm to close. Ran out of everything. Orders for products are done. Might need to buy extra milk from the warehouse club. Please order extra tomorrow morning.

Red Hat Group coming in on Friday. Reserve tables for 16.

Labor:
Josh will be in at 10 am tomorrow. Kudos to all who worked today – Karen, Jose, Patricia, Alex, Kelly, Greg, and Matt.

Jack's father is very ill. Leave Jack off the schedule for the next few days.

Issues:
OUT OF EVERYTHING! David pulled a no show today. Said his dad wouldn't let him come in because of the weather. He will be in at 6 am tomorrow. I called Wanda to come in at 6 am to help out with prep. Also, Alonso will be in at 6 am to help out.

Repairs and Maintenance:
Found leak in office wall and around freezer door. Looks like roof is leaking – will call landlord. Keep an eye on it.

Ice machine scheduled for routine maintenance on Friday.

Items Out of Stock: Low on dairy products. Check stock on coffee filters.

Marketing.

Franchisors can really be a good partner when they provide advertising or promotions to you. Most franchisors reserve a portion of your royalties for marketing/advertising efforts. Many will group franchises geographically to get more bang for their buck. This can be great if you are in a population dense area or it can be a disadvantage if you are in a more spread out geography where your customers may not see you as well. For example, if you are close to an area where two counties come together and the cable TV companies differ between counties and your franchisor wants to spend their (your) money on Cable TV ads, what if they choose the opposite cable company from where your location is serviced? If you are in a population dense area, then Cable TV ads may be out of the company's budget reach.

Even if the franchisor does some advertising/ promotions, you will still need to do your own and that costs money. With the advent of social media, a wise person will do whatever they can to leverage social media so that they can extend their advertising budget. But in addition to that, there is print media (newspapers, magazines), radio and television ads, billboards, and Internet advertising. There are coupons books to participate in, text coupons, and print coupons as well as Internet discount sites such as Groupon, Amazon Local and Living Social. You can collect email lists and send out information and newsletters. You can blog on your website and use keywords (words most often searched on the Internet) to help people locate you. Of course, the oldie but goodie – Word of Mouth is often the best bet for the cheapest way to bring people to you. On the Internet, it's called "going viral," but just having people talk about your business to their friends is gold.

If you are in a business that can participate in charitable events, you can build up customer goodwill by being involved in them as a sponsor or by donating items for their auctions. It's a great way to meet people outside of your usual customer base and to become known in the community. If you are receptive to helping out in the community you will be visited by lots of people looking for donations. If you constantly say no to everyone, you may generate ill will, if you constantly say yes to everyone, it can eat into your profit margins. Some owners believe that any donation should have a reciprocal component such as the charity mentioning your business in their ads or flyers. This isn't always practical. You may want to choose a certain type of foundation/charity to support such as cancer or children's charities. That way when someone asks for a donation but it doesn't fit into your guidelines you can honestly say that you already support several charities that fight cancer or whatever it is you support.

You will likely be visited by anyone in the media business. All the salespeople will be vying for your patronage. Rather than just tell them "no" right away, get to know them a bit and you may find out a wealth of information about what your competitors are doing and what the best deals are. If you are friendly to them, you can establish connections through them to other businesses and customers.

Being involved in galas or large benefit events can reach more people at one time than just a few. If your area has galas for cancer, AIDS, children's charities, etc. consider being a sponsor so that you get more exposure for less investment.

One of the biggest difficulties in putting on promotions is the length of time you need to plan for them. Often you need to order in special products, you need to contact the media for some press exposure, you need to put out special advertising which usually has to be in by the 10th of the month *before* the publication and you may need to have signs made, coupons printed, flyers distributed, social media posts coordinated or other things that just take time. You can't expect an event to be spectacular when it isn't planned correctly. Remember to allow yourself a few months before you want to do something so it is worth the time, effort and cost.

Finding out where your customers come from is invaluable since it lets you target a group rather than spreading your marketing dollars too thin. If you offer coded coupons or try different things like Groupon, Amazon Local, etc. you will know immediately where your customers came from. You'll know what discounts work and what doesn't. You may also find that you are more popular during different seasons of the years than others. You may find that if your location is busier in the winter because you are a vacation spot, them spending your dollars during that time may be more efficient just because your local population has swelled. The point is to spend your dollars where they bring you the best return.

⚜ ⚜ ⚜

Let me tell you more...

Many of the schools sell coupons books and restaurants play a big part in them. The kids sell them for about $30 and there are a few hundred coupons. The sales rep for the book asked me if I wanted to take part in the book. We only had to pay for a nominal charge since the books were being paid for by the schools that in turn would charge for them. I listened to the advice of the rep and make the coupon attractive enough to get people to actually visit us. Our deal was $5 off dinner for two. To my surprise there were over 1000 coupons redeemed in just one restaurant alone. That meant I had just given away $5000. Of course, there was no way to know how many of those that used the coupons were actually new customers or if there were customers that just hadn't been back in a while. Getting those types are worth the $5, but it is unlikely that the entire 1000 were worth the cost. The cost of that coupon was a loss to the business; it didn't just eat up the profit.

⚜ ⚜ ⚜

Commercial equipment costs lots more.
Commercial equipment is supposed to be much tougher than consumer equipment, however, the warranties may not be any better. For example, a commercial water heater which costs close to $8000 still has a five-year warranty. A commercial refrigerator may only have one year. Maintenance costs more, parts cost more and the equipment costs more. A piece of equipment may be a good deal new, but if your repairman has to drive two hours to work on it, you will have serious issues with the repair cost and the down time while you wait for it to be repaired.

After the warranties run out, the cost of repairs can increase yearly. When opening a new business, you must budget for increasing cost of repairs and even for replacement. Do your research and find out which brands of equipment have longer life and fewer repairs.

If a piece of equipment fails, you need to know immediately who to call for repair, how far away they are from your location, their expertise, if they stock parts, if you have a maintenance contract with them, is there a guaranteed response time and can they give you an estimate of the cost. Are they authorized to work on this brand? Sometimes, companies won't give you an estimate until they see the problem, but many can give you a "guestimate." If it is a critical piece of equipment, who can rent you a temporary replacement? Does another franchisee nearby have one you can borrow? Should you stock parts for this equipment? Always keep a repair log on each piece of equipment: record the date and time of repair, what was done and the cost. You will find it helpful in making decisions as to when to replace, rather than repair, a piece of equipment. You should also keep a file with all instructions for operating the equipment so other employees can access the file when needed (or even the repairman). Keep all models numbers and serial numbers in the file. Often, the repairperson will need this for warranty and parts information.

Warranties on some equipment, such as compressors, may require that you return the damaged equipment to get a refund. You need to keep track when it was sent back to the company and by whom, in case it gets lost. Keep the tracking number from a shipping company.

Leasing equipment may be an option. Beware of leasing equipment such as dishwashers that tie you into purchasing your dish chemicals from the same company at a higher cost than a competitor. In the long run, it still may be cost effective to lease equipment. Usually, repair costs are the problem of the company you have leased from and at the end of the term, you just give them the equipment back.

⚜ ⚜ ⚜

Let me tell you more…

We were required to use a piece of kitchen equipment that was not intended for the use we put it to. The franchisor would not let us use anything else although other competing chains had found ways around it. The franchisor continued to say they were investigating other choices. While we used the equipment, since it was used continually, we had to own more than one just to make sure that if we had a failure of the first on that we could still provide the customer with their food choice. That was an additional several thousand dollars in equipment cost. Also, when the equipment broke down, it was often $500-1000 every single service call because the equipment had an electronic component that would fail over and over. It was a continual source of profit drain.

Few things are worse than getting in your new order of food from the distributor and having your freezer fail. We learned that preventative maintenance on restaurant equipment was perhaps expensive but not as expensive as having something fail completely. We kept a laminated sheet on each cooler (refrigerator) and freezer and every morning a manager had to write down the temperature. Each piece of equipment had a thermometer in the door so it was an easy thing to do. Seeing a pattern of temperatures creeping upward usually meant you needed a service call so it was important to do the checking and notify other managers to keep a sharp eye out for any problems.

The main freezer failed one July leaving hundreds of products starting to thaw. The franchisor saved the day by allowing one of their refrigerated delivery tractor trailers to park in our delivery area and kept their refrigeration unit running 24 hours a day until we could get a new compressor for the freezer. We unloaded the freezer into the semi and the franchisor only charged us for gas and mileage to get the truck there. We still lost some of the product but were able to save the majority of it. The franchisor was a real hero that day.

⚜ ⚜ ⚜

Preventative Maintenance.

Preventative maintenance is performing routine maintenance before the equipment needs a repair. The purpose is to minimize failures, to keep the equipment running at its peak efficiency and to minimize downtime. As long as the money is available and a trustworthy, efficient repairman can perform the maintenance when you want it done (not getting in the way during your peak business hours) for a reasonable cost, it is a great idea.

Many companies will require that you sign a contract and either pay up front or quarterly or monthly. Make sure you get what you pay for. Does the contract include spare parts or just labor? What happens if the company you contracted with is sold and all the personnel changes? Can you still trust their expertise? If you are a contract maintenance customer, do you get priority when you have a system failure and need emergency service? Is there a guaranteed response time? Do you have time to check up on them to make sure they performed their scheduled maintenance? What happens when they don't have a part on their truck... will you have to pay for a return service call?

One of the frustrations of owning your own business is that it seems as if just when your business is running smoothly and making a profit, something breaks and requires a new investment. Knowing up front the expected life of your equipment will help you budget for replacement and determine if this business is really profitable.

Much of equipment maintenance involves, cleaning, lubricating, replacing filters, checking gauges, tightening connections, checking settings, etc. If you can train an employee to do the maintenance, you may save substantially. However, make sure the employee knows the safety issues involved and knows when to get a certified technical rep involved. Never let an employee that doesn't have good decision-making skills work on equipment!

Equipment contingencies.

If equipment is critical to doing business you must have a contingency plan for each piece. Look at the amount of business you would lose if you have an equipment failure, and then do some research. If your equipment fails, what is the most likely component to fail? Would a repairman keep that component on his truck? Would it need to be shipped in from the manufacturer? What is the shipping time? Where would a repairman have to travel from and how long would it take? Assume that the part would have to be shipped in and it would take two to three days. Can you run your business for three days without this equipment? Can you rent a replacement? If not, then do you need to have a back up piece of equipment? What would the cost be to keep one on hand? Do you have a place to keep it? The cost of lost business is not only the business you lost during your equipment failure, but also the lost FUTURE business of customers that were upset and decided to never come back.

You must look at the cost to carry a replacement piece of equipment of find out if one would be available to rent in the case of failure. If the cost is absolutely too high, then you must have an emergency plan in place to minimize downtime. Have emergency phone numbers pasted on the equipment. Let employees know who to call for service if you, as the owner, cannot be reached. Make sure you have backup service companies.

Systems and schedules.

The easiest way to make a business "run itself" is to create systems and schedules. The more routine a business becomes, the less people required to run it, the more smoothly each day goes and the greater chance profit can be maximized. People work better when they know what is expected and what is coming up. There is less discussion needed, fewer things to be learned and less likelihood of a crisis.

Employees should know their work schedule as soon as possible for the week ahead. They should know what day of the week is special for any certain task. If they know before they walk in the door that inventory is done on Saturday or the last day of the month, they're already thinking of what needs to be done before they walk in the door.

An employee that has a checklist to perform his job, especially opening and closing functions that have to do with cash handling, cleaning or securing a building will not have an excuse to forget anything. You can hold them accountable by having a laminated checklist that is signed and dated each day. If a task is forgotten then you can look at the checklist and see what employee signed it but didn't actually perform all the functions.

Any schedules posted should only allow changes by designated managers or employees. If a change is made, then it should be noted and initialed for accountability. For example, if you post an employee work schedule and two employees agree to switch shifts, unless an authorized manager approves it you may have an employee substituting for another that cannot do what needs to be done. Suppose a minor cannot handle dangerous equipment or that there would be less coverage because the substitute has not been trained on all the areas that the original employee was. These are decisions that affect customer service and profits so only someone aware of all the implications should make the final approval.

Monthly Cleaning Checklist
Sample for a Restaurant

Creating a checklist
1. Create a series of steps for a repetitive task
2. Add a place where a person will initial the checklist when they complete the job
3. Save it on the computer so it can be changed as needed
4. Print it out and laminate it
5. Put it on a clipboard and tie a china marker to the clip
6. Have the employee check off each task, initial it and date it so you can check that all is complete
7. Wipe it off for the next time with a paper towel and use again

Monthly Cleaning List (For end of month)

____Scrub the front and back sidewalks with deck brush and soapy water.

____Deep clean the cooking equipment with brushes and soapy water.

____Spray down, clean off, and dry out all rubber mats.

____Make sure all ceiling vents in the dining room and the back of the house are clean.

____Check filters on the ice machine and clean the vents.

____Clean and spray down the black bakery display racks. Dry well.

____Organize shelves in the prep area and the dry storage/employee shelf area.

____Clean area by the water heater, move shelves, clean the floors and walls.

____Spot clean the walls.

____Plane and bleach all the cutting boards. Then run through the dishwasher.

____Pull weeds from the sidewalk and the patio areas

DATE: INITIALS:

Leaving an audit trail.

In every business there must be a system of checks and balances. This means that for every procedure, there is a way to check for accuracy with a different system. A Point of Sale system will record each sale, list it as cash, check or charge, and at the end of the day, show you how much money you should have to deposit in the bank.

To check the accuracy of cash handling procedures, you would count out the cash drawers (leaving any money that you use in the drawers to make change and was in the drawer before you began to make sales), combine all the cash and then compare it to the POS computer report to make sure that it is the same. Most POS systems will also tell you based on the sales and type of sales how much money should be in each cash drawer. So if you have an employee assigned to a specific register and the register's money drawer is counted down at the end of the employee's shift and compared to the POS computer report, you will immediately know how accurate the employee was at making change. If there is more than just a few cents discrepancy, then you need to look at theft, giving out the wrong change or other issues such as giving away free products to their friends.

Never allow only one person to be responsible for all the cash. There should always be someone looking over his or her shoulder. Almost every business owner will at some point experience employee theft in some way. It can be as small as an employee giving a friend an unearned discount or as large as embezzlement of thousands. Finding it and stopping it immediately have to do with the systems and audit trails you have put in place. Often it depends on other employees telling you that something is not right. They have noticed something or seen suspicious behavior. If your employees are treated well and loyal to you, they will tell you instead of letting it go and not caring.

Food/product cost.

Fast food franchises are famous for knowing down to the penny what it cost for a French fry to hit the floor. Their production systems are so finely honed that they know exactly what it cost in labor for the person in the drive through to get their order in two minutes time versus three.

Know exactly what it costs to produce your product, what it takes in labor costs to sell it and how much waste you will have if it doesn't sell. Some products have a higher profit margin than others. Customers may perceive it as having a higher value and thus pay more for it. This means that it might benefit you to "push" that product more and achieve a higher return on investment.

Placing orders.

There is normally a cutoff time for orders to be placed to make sure the products you need are loaded onto the truck. Most ordering systems now are online but there will still be that last minute item that you suddenly need an extra case of and have to get a real person at the distribution center to help you with. Do they have someone answering the phone at all hours? Will they be helpful or make you life difficult?

Even if your inventory system keeps track of the products used, there is still waste and shrinkage that won't be accounted for. A real live person needs to master the art of taking inventory and deciding, based on your forecast, just how much of each product you will need. If you are a restaurant and have several different vendors such as a fresh produce vendor, a dairy vendor, as well as the franchisor's products, it can get complicated. Also, if you have to deal with taking inventory in a freezer and walk in cooler, it is even harder since no one wants to be in that environment for long.

Checking in an order.

In a busy restaurant, you may have deliveries of produce daily, deliveries from the franchisor once or twice a week and other commodity deliveries (paper goods, cleaning supplies, etc.) at other times. Sometimes, the supplier wants to deliver during your busy time and you cannot possibly make sure the delivery is put away correctly or check in the order to see if you received exactly what you ordered. Hopefully, your suppliers are good but mistakes happen and sometimes they happen a lot. Some vendors want to just stack the boxes and leave but you still have to work around the mess and often cannot get to what you need.

When we took delivery from the franchisor or distributor that carried in their products, often the invoices would be twelve or more pages long with hundreds of items involved. We had to dedicate one extra employee just to check in the items because we had to let the supplier know on the spot if we were shorted an item or if an item was delivered by mistake. Not knowing could cost an extra $50 or more. If it were a critical item, the supplier would have to overnight freight us the missing box, at their cost. Having to have that extra employee was a higher cost to us because the supplier never showed up at the same time, depending on how many other deliveries they had. If you have items that need to be in the freezer or cooler, you must hustle to receive all your items quickly so there is no degradation of the product quality.

Your liability.

Anything that you sell can be the subject of a product liability suit. Basically, the law requires that you take all due care possible to avoid harm or injury to a consumer. Even if you manufacture or produce your product with all caution to avoid such injury, the misuse by a consumer can still cause a lawsuit.

The suit against McDonald's by a woman that burned her thigh with a hot cup of coffee and won her claim is famous. Supposedly, she put the cup between her legs to open it while she was a passenger in a car and the coffee splashed her legs. She was burned and the fabric of her pants held the hot coffee next to her skin, allowing the burn to be much more serious. Maybe she didn't use common sense but McDonald's still got sued because the temperature tested in the store was higher than most fast food restaurants. If you saw the picture of her burns, you would likely be horrified too. They have since reduced the temperature of their coffee.

You can never tell what a consumer will do so you must adequately warn them of any potential danger as well as make all efforts to protect them. Also, a consumer is much more likely to spread negative reviews of your business than good reviews. So, always be aware of what could happen and be forewarned. If you have to cover yourself legally with diplomatic warnings, than do so. If you serve hot coffee, then tell your customer, "Be careful, it's very hot." If you serve a very spicy food, than let the customer know before he/she orders it. If you sell a product that, when used improperly could injure someone, then educate your customers as to the proper procedure. One lawsuit could wipe out your business, even if you didn't do anything wrong, so make an effort to be extra careful.

If a customer does come to you with a problem, you should always apologize for the inconvenience. This can be done without taking blame for a problem (if you really didn't cause the problem), but a customer always wants to know that they are important to you and that their business is welcome. You should ask questions as to the nature of the problem, which shows your interest and you can offer to exchange the product, refund their money and even give them something for free. Anything you do to make them happy will prevent a disgruntled customer from telling all their friends about their unpleasant experience.

Often, just having a sincere apology is all a customer needs but it is always best to go the extra mile. If a customer is truly injured in your place of business or by your product, you will need to offer them medical care. Let your insurance company know immediately if you will have a claim.

Most often, a customer just wants to know that someone really cares if the product they received is defective, if they hurt themselves on the business's premises, or that their satisfaction matters. Let every customer know you care by listening to them, paraphrasing what you are hearing and saying it back to them, asking them what will make them a satisfied customer and negotiate if need be. If you promise them something, follow through with your promise.

Accounting practices.

It is tempting in a busy day to put off inputting data into your accounting system, or to push it to the side because of more important things. This can mean a monumental job once you finally begin the process.

Whether or not you have a point of sale system that accumulates your sales information, you will need to maintain an accounting system, which allows you to calculate your profit and loss at any point in time so you know where your business stands. It is a compilation of your sales, receivables, expenses, payables, general ledger transactions, checks written and depreciation and amortization.

As a small business owner, you will need a way to input all the information mentioned above into a software package such as QuickBooks. Initially, you set up a chart of accounts that will include:

1. Asset accounts, which are what you own that can be converted to cash, or is cash
2. Inventory
3. Accounts receivable and prepaid expenses
4. Liability accounts which are obligations you have to meet including accounts payables, loans and interest owed
5. Equity accounts, which is the investment to open the business plus any retained earnings added to the account
6. Revenue accounts such as sales or interest income
7. Expense accounts that are the day-to-day and month-to-month expenses you pay for utilities, the cost of goods, insurance, rent, etc.
8. Any *contra- accounts* such as amortization and depreciation, which are deductions from your profit allowing for a regulated reduction in the value of your equipment and building if you own it (depreciation) or non-tangible assets (amortization)

Once you have your chart of accounts, every time you make a general ledger transaction, you will be choosing which account to charge the expense or income against. To keep your accounting system in balance, it is important to be consistent and keep meticulous records. The more detailed the chart of accounts, the better you are able to see where you are spending money and control it. If you want to keep tabs on a particular expense such as coffee used in the employee kitchen, then you can name an account "coffee for employees". The data is only as good as the input so you must always put expenditures for employee coffee into that account. If you forget you have this account and input the expenditure into a miscellaneous account, then you will not have a full accounting for employee coffee.

In a system such as QuickBooks, you will have check registers set up for your bank accounts and each time you write a check, you will record it in the check register. At the bottom of the check line will be another line for the account that the amount paid is going towards. So if you write a check for the coffee that is going into the employee kitchen, then the account you fill in would be "coffee for employees". What you are doing is crediting your bank account and debiting the "coffee for employee" account. In a computerized system it is not necessary to make the differentiation for credits and debits because it does it for you. When you set up the chart of accounts, each account became a certain type and will function according to the type of account it is. You should know the difference between the terms and learn this by a basic accounting course or book.

Even if you have a point of sale system, you will need to transfer the sales figure from your POS to your accounting system. Whether you do it daily, weekly, or monthly depends on the volume and how closely you need to monitor your profit and loss. Again, here is where self discipline comes in and knowing that the sooner you input data, the faster you will find a problem if there is one. If you know quickly that your sales are good but that your profit isn't what you hoped it would be, you can check your expenses to see where you have overspent and change it before you go seriously off kilter.

Your accountant.

Choosing a good accountant is like choosing a partner for your business. You will want to have a long-term relationship with him/her because it makes transitions easier from year to year and will cost you less in consultation fees as the accountant becomes more familiar with your business.

Ask other business owners for referrals. Interview the accountant and make sure that you feel they can give you the time you deserve, that they will listen to your needs, that you feel they base their fees fairly, and that they will stand by you in case you are audited. A Certified Public Accountant has to pass tests and keep up with new accounting and tax laws. Find out how long they have been in business and if they have experience working with other business owners similar to your industry.

Accountants can make mistakes. Don't just sign any tax documents or forms without looking over them and asking questions. They may have differing ideas on what should be classified in different accounts, which can affect your taxes. Ask questions and learn from them. The more you know, the less money you will have to spend on an accountant and the more you can do yourself.

Cash flow.

You can still be a profitable business but have no cash in which to pay invoices. This happens when you have a high amount of receivables that customers have not paid. This is one reason to stay on top of all money that people owe you. You cannot pay your own bills if you don't have cash in the bank. That is why you will hear the term cash flow. Cash flow also means that it is the profit you have made or money taken in *before* depreciation and amortization reduces it. If you are collecting sales tax, you in effect have a flow of cash coming in but it is being held in escrow for the payment of the sales tax at the end of the month. Don't forget that this is not your money.

Tracking when your deposits are available to your bank account is necessary to make sure an adequate amount of money is there to pay your invoices. In any business, there is constantly cash flowing in and cash flowing out. The more you can put aside a reserve of cash, the less vigilant you have to be about watching the flow in an out.

Documentation for taxes.

Even though you have accounting software you will still need to maintain and document all deductions for business expenses. This means that every time you buy office supplies, light bulbs, and janitorial supplies and pay an invoice, you must file the receipt away so you can show proof in case you are ever audited. Your accountant will advise you on all the legitimate deductions you can take to reduce the taxes you owe. Different accountants have different philosophies on the risk you can take on a deduction.

Sales tax.

Collecting and paying sales tax is one area that you want to stay on top of at all times. Each state differs on what goods sales tax is collected on. Some of it is open for interpretation but if the state audits you and differs from your viewpoint you could end up paying lots of back taxes and penalties. For example, in my state food in a restaurant is taxed, however, food that you cannot consume on the premises is not. So, if someone orders his or her food "to go", then how do you judge this gray area? Some restaurants will not charge tax on to go orders and some will charge tax to protect themselves from sales tax audits. Some will charge tax on to go orders but not charge tax on items such as a loaf of bread which would be unlikely to be eaten on the premises.

Usually, states will collect the sales tax monthly. You are responsible for filing and paying the tax on time. It is your responsibility as the business owner to find out how to file and pay your tax. Penalties for late payments can be steep. In my state, you must file for a sales tax number before you can begin to collect taxes. There is a standard state sales tax and then each county charges an additional small amount which also must be collected, however, all payments go to the state and the state then pays the counties. In my state, the current state tax rate is 6% and a county may charge one half to one percent or more in additional tax.

Once you have your sales tax number, you will collect the tax based on the location of the business. This is the physical location of the business and if you have multiple locations, the rate may differ among the locations. Check with your state to determine its laws. Be aware that when you collect tax, your cash flow will be more than you've actually made because you must hold this money in escrow until the end of the month when you have to pay the state. In my state, you have ten days after the end of the month to file your report showing your sales, any exempt sales such as nontaxable items, and the amount of sales tax you owe, with the amount you owe the state and the county broken out. My state also gives you a $30 a month credit for your troubles of filing and paying.

Some states will allow you to file and pay your tax via the mail, but once you reach a certain level in taxes owed, accumulated by the first year in business, then all subsequent taxes must be paid by the Internet. This means filling out an "e-form" and then filling in your bank account information and giving permission to have the amount debited out of the account.

My state gives you a one time per year forgiveness for filing late or making a mistake on your "e-form". After that, you must pay penalties, which are ten percent of what you owed. So, if you are a business paying in $5000 per month, this is a substantial penalty of $500 for being late or making an error.

Most businesses that use a Point of Sale system that is computer automated, has the sales tax built into the programming for collection. Each transaction is recorded and the tax will be shown on an end of the month report. Usually, the company that has sold you the computer POS system will input the correct sales tax percentage, however any new start up business should check for the next month, calculating manually a few of the transactions, to see if the system is indeed automatically collecting the correct tax. For example, if they input 6.5% into your system and you owe 7%, the state will hold you accountable for the full 7% which means you just lost a half of a percent of your sales from your bottom line profit.

Depreciation.

Depreciation is an allowable deduction from your tax liability. The government gives schedules for different items as to the amount of time you can take to fully depreciate it. A building is depreciated over 39 years (but the land is not depreciated) while a piece of equipment is depreciated over varying numbers of years depending on what it is. A computer may be written off as an expense or depreciated over six years while office equipment, including furniture, requires 10 years to write off. However, the schedules of allowable depreciation *can change*. That is why an accountant is so valuable. They keep up with all the tax law changes.

The deduction of depreciation is a very valuable thing. It allows you to earn money and reduce the profit shown at year-end by the amount of depreciation. Thus, you also reduce your taxes.

Petty cash accounting.

When you have a business where managers and other employees might have expenses, then you must find a way to keep track of what they spend, any cash advanced and receipts for their purchases and expenses. If you send an employee out to buy an emergency supply of paper towels, usually the manager takes cash from your safe. You need to have a slip filled out that records who has the money, when it was given, and for what amount. A shortage in a safe can mean theft, so to prevent anyone from becoming alarmed or someone being accused unfairly, some type of audit trail is essential. Once the employee returns with the change, then the slip should be removed but be kept in the records. The cost of the paper towels needs to be recorded as an expense.

Some point of sale systems have ways to record an advance on money. This way the employee would have been given money out of a register where an authorized individual would use their key card to open the drawer and input the information on the register who took what amount of money and what the expenditure is for.

If you use a company credit card to buy supplies, many credit card companies will itemize all purchases for an entire year at the end of each year. This also gives you an additional audit trail and a record of what was purchased for your accounting detail.

Always have a safe place to keep receipts for anything that you don't write out a check. The receipt is your proof to the government that the deduction on your taxes was real. You should make short notes on receipts where the item purchases is not readily clear. Also, at the end of the accounting period when you are entering the expenses into the software system, then it speeds up the time necessary to figure out what the receipt was for and what account needs to be debited.

Different owners have different views about their level of risk for allowable expenses. Discuss with your accountant just what allowable expenses are. Many people write off the expense to own a car if they use it for business purposes, however, it is not usually that cut and dried. If you also use the car to drive to and from work, then the miles driven for just personal use may not be an allowable expense.

⚜ ⚜ ⚜

Let me tell you more...

One employee informed me just after he was hired and the paperwork was filled out and submitted that he was diabetic and had an insulin pump. He did not have to disclose it before hand, by law, however, it was frustrating to watch him drink soda all day and do things that were detrimental to his health. He would sometimes miss work because of his illness but was still a good employee. During his tenure, we often had little shortages of petty cash, which would mysteriously show back up a day or so later. He had some turmoil in his personal life when his girlfriend became pregnant unexpectedly.

The missing money continued to happen quite a bit and it was fairly obvious he was the culprit. Since he continued to pay it back and none of it ever came up missing for longer periods of time, I let it slide but kept an eye on him, auditing the money and deposits much more carefully after he had been alone in the office. When he finally left my employ, the safe actually ended up being "over" the standard amount so I figured he had paid back his "borrowing" with interest, to the tune of $100 extra.

⚜ ⚜ ⚜

Accounts payable.

Accounts payable are those invoices for goods and services that you owe to others. Never assume that you are being invoiced correctly but always check the prices guaranteed and the invoice numbers. Accounts Payable Accountants and Auditors make a lot of income by saving a company money. They do this by making sure the promised costs were billed and not increased, by making sure duplicate invoices are not paid again and by making sure that all early payment discounts are taken advantage of.

When you receive an invoice, for a business such as a restaurant, it may be fourteen pages long. This means it is time consuming and can be annoying to check every line item, however, if you don't, you will inevitably lose money. When you receive a shipment, you should take the bill of lading or invoice that comes with the order and first check to make sure that you did receive all the goods on the bill. If a driver is waiting for you to check the order in, circle the item, make him sign the bill that the item is missing and keep a copy and send one back with him. Maintain a log of any missing items so you can check to make sure you received a credit or the item. In a business with hundreds of products going in and out this is crucial.

Many invoices have a "pay by" date, which shows you when the bill is due. If the bill is paid early and gives a discount, take advantage of that if possible. If you can't make a payment, then pay even a small amount to show good faith or call the vendor and make arrangements. If you don't communicate, you could just suddenly stop receiving shipments, which will impact your sales if you have no product to sell.

Save all of the statements and invoices that you have paid in a file for each vendor. On each invoice write the date it was paid and the check number. Vendors can come back after you for up to five years for unpaid invoices. In five years, will you remember if you paid or not? Make sure you have proof that you have. This is an unfortunate part of our legal system that you should have to provide proof, but that's the way it is right now. A vendor might lose their payment records and decide to turn your invoice over to a collection agency when they audit their records.

Utilities usually make you deposit funds in an escrow account so that if you don't pay your bill, they can still be paid. In a business, this deposit can be thousands of dollars, which means the utility company is holding the money that you could be using to pay others or invest in equipment. An insurance company will sell you a bond that you pay a few hundred dollars for and that insures the utility company their invoice will be paid instead of requiring the deposit. The insurance company will probably require your financial records each year to renew the bond. Suppose the utility company requires a $4000 bond for electricity (a restaurant can use thousands of dollars of electricity per month) or you can pay an insurance company $350 per year for a bond that covers the deposit. This would mean that you would have the use of the remaining money for several years before you would end up spending the $4000. The only thing to be wary of is that at the end of the term, when you close your business, you should receive the deposit back, whereas, with the insurance bond, the money is spent and can't be returned.

Audit trails are one of those things that get pushed to the side when things get busy. It's easy to forget to document transactions when you are pushed for time, however, it's also one of those things that is worth its weight in gold when you do have a problem and can trace the origin of the problem easily. An audit trail simply means that you have more than one way to find information. You can work backwards or forwards to find it. It means that there is a common sense way to find data in more than one location. It is a record of changes, transactions, communications, and activities.

For example, a vendor notifies you that you have not made a payment on an invoice. You check your bank register to see if there is a check with their name on it and look at the visual image your bank provides online to see if the correct invoice number is written on it. Perhaps the invoice number is one digit off because there was an error in copying the check number. You provide the company with the check number and let them know it has the incorrect invoice number written on it and they should apply it to the correct invoice. Problem solved. Or perhaps you cannot find a record of a check written for this company in the time frame. So you go to the vendor file and find the invoice and see if you have written "Paid" on the invoice with the date and check number and then find the check that way. These are examples of audit trails.

A vendor can still legally come after you to pay an invoice five years later. If you don't have the information that you have paid, how will you fight it? It seems ridiculous that this can happen, but it does. Be prepared.

⚜ ⚜ ⚜

Let me tell you more...

When you sign a contract with a vendor, you may have a separate salesperson and service person or you may have a service person who also sells the contract. With a linen service we used, the salesperson contracted that they would supply us with rugs for the dining room and rubber mats for the kitchen are. The service people picked up the rugs to take back to their company's location where they would be cleaned and sanitized and at the same time they would put down a clean set. This meant for any logo requirements, there needed to be two sets of rugs and mats. The service person would come in and often "forget" to change out all the rugs and only change out a partial set, although we were still charged for the full amount. This meant trying to watch them carefully and follow behind them to make sure they were doing what they promised, difficult to do in a busy place.

Chemical supplies were also another area where the servicemen would leave invoices for chemicals they replaced at the mop sink, but unless you watched them do it, it was difficult to tell if there was truly a new gallon of chemicals hooked up to the sink or not. It wasn't a situation where you could easily take it down to check on its volume or see through the container.

One of the vendors that gave poor service refused to cancel my agreement. They continually shorted me on my service and so I told them to cancel my agreement. They cited the small print on the back of the agreement which said they could enforce their contract for five years. It was my fault for not reading all the fine print. I liked the original salesperson (who left) and trusted him (again my fault). The new sales person was very adamant and he absolutely refused to cancel the contract no matter how poor their service. After going round and round with him we agreed to meet and discuss it in person. Utilizing a piece of advice I had received from another female business owner, I had a recording device on the table with us and told him that I had a poor memory so I wanted to record our conversation. Immediately, he was nervous and shifted uncomfortably. He was much more civil and when I told him that social media was a great way for people to spread the word about a poor experience with a vendor, he finally capitulated and canceled the agreement.

⚜ ⚜ ⚜

Receivables.

When someone owes you money, you must stay on top of it to collect what you are owed. An automatic invoicing system that ages the payments and prints out statements is best. You should have a policy that a statement is sent out every month or in the case of a perishable item, where it will be consumed and cannot be returned, perhaps every two weeks. Customers that you depend upon for a large percentage of sales need to be treated with respect and appreciation, however, it also means you are dependent on them for your cash flow and profit. If they begin to have financial problems, you need to set limits of credit that you will give them before letting it affect your own business.

Most businesses will have patterns of payments. Some pay immediately, some wait a few weeks and some pay monthly. If you notice a change in their payment patterns, especially if the time between payments is extended, then you need to do some research to see what is happening to the company by searching the web. Look for new management (perhaps you need to make a sales call), issues in their industry, or any news about layoffs. This will give you a clue about what action to take or whether they need to be monitored more closely.

Extending credit/ invoicing.

Any customer that you will be extending credit to, should fill out a credit application whether you intend to check their credit rating or not. The application should have all the relevant information of name, address, phone numbers, contact information and references. In case you have trouble collecting a debt, then at least you have contact information on file. It also shows that you are monitoring your receivables.

Most credit checks will cost you money so you need to determine if it is worth the cost. Most small businesses will extend a certain amount of credit to most other businesses, but not individuals. You can protect yourself when extending credit to granting a probationary period where invoices need to be paid in a week instead of thirty days or put a limit on the amount of credit that a business can have open at any one time. Any time you take an order it would be necessary to check the company's outstanding invoices to see if they are near their limit.

Your bank.

Your relationship with a bank is important. If you handle large amounts of cash, although it would seem that a bank would like to receive your cash, they may not. Some banks look at the amount of time a teller takes to work through your transactions so if you make them count several thousand dollars or add up lots of rolled coins, the bank may charge you a cash handling fee. You've taken up too much time with their tellers. Some banks will charge you a fee of ten cents for every roll of pennies you make them handle. So they just took twenty percent of your profits just from your pennies!

A bank may also hold your check deposits until they clear from the bank they were written on. This means the money is not available for you to earn interest or pay or bills. Having a close relationship with a bank means that they waive this procedure and allow the money to be deposited at the end of the day, when the computers are updated.

If you deposit more than $10,000 in a day then the bank must fill out paperwork showing your tax I.D. to confirm that you are a legitimate business and not doing something illegal. This takes up a lot of time and puts all your information on record.

Handling sums of cash should also make you aware of what and who is around you at all times when leaving your business and driving to the bank. Is it safe to carry it in a briefcase? Do you need a transportation service which costs money? If you need lots of coin for change, you may need to pre-order the amount because many banks do not keep large amounts of rolled coin on hand. Varying your banking times can keep you safer because people will not see a pattern and expect you. When depositing cash, do not talk about your business in front of strangers at the bank.

Banks also charge a fee if the deposit is off from what the deposit slip says even if the teller counted it and confirmed the amount. The deposit goes through another process of verification and if it is found to be off at this point, then a fee is usually automatic.

As a business owner, you must decide whether to allow employees to take the deposit to the bank. If it is large sums of cash, you have to take into account both safety for the employee and the deposit as well as the possibility of theft. Deposits also need to be verified before leaving the business. Some businesses have a closing manager and an opening manager both count the deposit, however, if there is a problem at the bank and money is short, then who do you blame? Another way is to have the closing manager put the deposit in a sealed envelope and not open it until it is at the bank. This means that you don't have time to alleviate any issues with incorrect counting, and may be charged a fee from the bank if they have to correct it.

Credit cards.

The world of credit cards has become a never-ending source of issues. Merchants need to take several kinds of credit cards (i.e. Visa, Mastercard, Discover, American Express) and if you don't, it is likely that someone will complain that they don't own the cards you accept. The more cards you process, the better the rates you will have to pay as a processing charge. Different kinds of cards (i.e. cards that accumulate free airline miles, etc.) will make you pay more. When a customer uses this type of card, you pay more to the credit card processor. International credit cards also charge you more. The fee structure is usually set up where you pay a standard charge for each card and then pay an additional fee as to the type of card. You don't have much choice since you can't control what card a customer uses other than the actual category such as Visa. Different credit card processors offer you different rates, however, almost all of them go through the same few databanks so you are really using the same service.

When credit cards are swiped through a point of sale system, it is immediately sent over the Internet to be validated. If your point of sale system is down, or you have computer errors, you must process cards the old fashioned way by making an imprint or by writing down the number and running them through the computer/point of sale later. This means you take on the risk of having a card declined. It is too late then to get the customer to pay in a different way.

Merchant services account.

When you accept credit cards, you will sign a contract with a credit card processing company. This is called having a merchant account. Most of these companies are go-betweens with one or two large processors. The company will charge you rates based on the type of business you are, the amount of credit per transaction (sales), and the total amount of credit you will be funneling though their company. Most charge a standard rate per each transaction and then an additional amount based on the type of credit card that is used. A credit card that has all sorts of perks such as giving away prizes or airline miles will cost you, as a merchant, more than other cards. Overall, the approximate amount that you will lose by taking credit cards is somewhere around 3% of your sales, depending on volume. You will also be charged additional fees if the card was not magnetically swiped but just the number was entered. Depending on the type of business you are, using a debit card that requires a PIN number may also charge you additional fees. Many businesses prefer to run a debit card as if it was a credit card for this reason.

Your point of sale system will show that the sale was with a credit or debit card. The customer signs a receipt so you have proof of his permission to be charged. In certain businesses, such as fast food, charges under a certain amount do not need a signature. The credit transactions will show up on reports on the point of sale system.

Most credit card processors will process the batch of credit card transactions for a business at the end of each night. At the time of the sale, the card is "pre-authorized" but there is no actual money exchange until it is batched in the evening all at once. The processor may deposit the money for your charges the following day or it may take one or two days. The sooner the money is deposited into your bank account, the sooner you can make use of it, so this is an important point to consider when checking out processors. Usually, at the end of the month, all fees will be deducted from your last transactions and it will reduce your deposits.

If you run through lots of credit transactions, at the end of the month you may get a printout of more than twenty pages. By the sheer volume of transactions, it is almost impossible to audit and check each one. You should, however, make a practice of randomly checking these reports to see if you are being charged the fees that were agreed upon. Also, at the renewal of your contract you should check other companies and compare fee structures. Most processors are aggressively competitive in their rates and there is a bit of wiggle room.

⚜ ⚜ ⚜

Let me tell you more…

The fastest growing crime in the United States today is identity theft. It has gotten so commonplace that you will find that most organizations that deal with it have a blasé attitude.

There is also a new twist on identity theft for small business owners. Identity thieves are stealing corporate identification numbers and setting up credit card processing accounts. They can then process thousands of stolen credit card numbers through this account, have the money deposited into their bank account and then close out the account and move on. They also may be selling a fictitious product on the Internet and never shipping anything so they can process the credit cards.

I came home from work to find a package on my doorstep from a credit card processing company "welcoming" me as a new account holder. It was addressed to a woman I have never heard of and also in my real company name (but one that doesn't process credit cards). I called the bank and was told that my "assistant" opened the account for me. The supposed assistant also gave her own address and a 1-800 number for the account. Because it really was a legitimate business (mine) they shipped the welcome package to the *real* corporate address (mine). The woman turned out to be fictitious as well as her address. The phone number worked for a few days and account was opened *over the phone.* I called the credit card processing company and spent hours on the phone with them. The account had been opened a week before and had processed thousands of dollars of credit cards already. The account was finally shut down and I breathed a sigh of relief. That was on a Friday.

I filed a police report and began the search to find out what else I needed to do to protect myself. A detective for the police department told me that there are over 100 million credit card transactions per day and of those about *1 million* are fraudulent. We, as consumers and merchants, end up paying the bill in high transaction fees or interest rates.

On Monday, I came home to find *another* welcome package from *another* credit card processor. I called immediately and shut down that account. Because the package arrived so quickly, no credit cards had been processed. Remember, the first account was shut down on Friday and within hours a new one was opened with a different processor. The new processor's security specialist was the first person in all this mess to tell me everything that needed to be done. She also told me that the person opening the account had given them not only my corporate identification number but also my social security number. That was very alarming.

Soon after, the bank account the fictitious woman set up was located in New Jersey. That set up another set of problems because the local sheriff's department does not have jurisdiction there. I filed a report with the Federal Trade Commission, the IRS and issued fraud alerts to all three credit-reporting agencies (Equifax, Trans Union and Experian). I took out identity theft insurance through a credit reporting agency (about $100). I was told that I could never change my social security number unless I was in a victim witness protection program.

I went back to the original account processor and finally spoke to *their* security specialist. She informed me that three other legitimate companies in the Southeast also had their identities used to set up fraudulent accounts at the same time. The specialist knew immediately that these were fraudulent accounts (and realized it at the same time I received my first welcome kit) because all the companies were processing the *same* credit card numbers and none of the credit cards had actually been "presented" to the supposed merchant. They were stolen numbers. She was able to back out all the entries to the bank account and recover all the money. What a relief. The person used several different banks in different locations.

After speaking to many different people I discovered that we all need to assume our identities have *already* been used or stolen. Lots of identity thieves are overseas and use the Internet to perform the crime. It is virtually impossible now to make sure that everyone that sees your personal information actually keeps it safe. Of course, I had to determine where my information could have been stolen because the thief need both the company IRS federal identification number as well as my social security number. The only companies to have that information were my bank and my payroll company.

Automatic bank drafts.

Most franchisors write into their contract that you must pay your royalties by automatic withdrawals from your bank account. Anytime you give someone access to your banking information, you are opening yourself up to possible mistakes that can cost you money. If you cannot control when a withdrawal is made (even if it is within a two day window) you cannot make sure that there is enough money to cover the amount.

Sharing your bank account information with anyone and authorizing a withdrawal on a continuing basis can be harmful to your business. Use the utmost care in making this decision. Withdrawals that are made without you having to give your permission can result in overdraft fees and difficulty in stopping the withdrawals.

If you have a bank account that offers the service of "Bill Pay" then you can pay bills online and make sure that an invoice is paid on time and you will know exactly when the money will be taken out of your account.

Using a money scale.

A great checks and balance feature to have is an electronic money scale. The money scale costs about $400 and is worth its weight in gold. Small and compact, it sits on a desk and will weigh accurately dollar bills, loose change and rolled coins. It also has the option of adding up the money you are weighing and running an adding machine type of receipt. The receipt should be included in anything you count such as the bank deposit and cash register drawers.

Any business that handles a lot of cash as opposed to credit card transactions, will have other considerations in fees. The fees include transportation to the bank for the deposits and receiving change; handling fees from the banks for the cash, and the lost time it takes to be going to and from the bank as well as the time you spend waiting for a teller.

Creating written policies.

Policies are necessary not just because of federal laws regarding discrimination, but because you should always have policies in place for your work environment to be a cooperative situation where your employees feel protected in the workplace. There can be liability involved if you don't do this, but it is just good business to do it too. Employees that feel you have their best interests at heart are loyal and hard working. They will give you their best efforts. This means monitoring how employees interact, how managers treat their employees and how employees treat their managers and also by listening to not just *what is said*, but *HOW* it is said.

All policies dealing with employees should be standardized and put in writing. This protects you as a business by showing you have policies in compliance with the laws and also ensures that you treat all employees in a similar manner.

Some of the areas where you need to create a standard, enforceable policy are about hiring practices, discrimination, late arrivals, calling in sick (who to talk to, when to do it, sufficient notice, etc.), vacation time and pay, health insurance, days off, employee discounts, privacy policies, right to search personal belongings (in case of substance abuse), injury procedures, probation periods, what constitutes an offense for immediate dismissal, pay periods, overtime, breaks, who can give discounts or void out a sale and just about anything else you can think of.

Vendor agreements.

Some vendors will require service agreements or contracts. If you want to lease clean throw rugs or if you want a service to monitor your cleaning chemicals and automatically refill them and bill you, you will most likely have to make a commitment to the company as to the frequency of service and the length of the term. Just because the company promised you a certain level service doesn't mean you will get it. You should educate your employees and make sure you get what you paid for. Don't just assume that because you like the serviceman that you are getting everything you've paid for. Who will make sure that the vendor supplies all the contracted for services or products if you are not there? Mistakes happen. If you have spent time negotiating a contract with a vendor, it will only be cost effective if the vendor lives up to their end of the bargain.

Usually a sales person is involved in the initial contracting phase and then a different area of the company takes over. A sales person may tell you things to make the sale. No matter how friendly you are with them, no matter how believable they are, get the offer in writing and make sure that any exceptions to their standard contract are noted and signed. If the contract says (read ALL the small print) that the term is for five years but the salesperson says you may cancel at any time, get it signed by an authorized company representative. Don't ever take their word for it. They may not be working for the vendor a year from now.

⚜ ⚜ ⚜

Let me tell you more…

One of the subcontractors that franchisor wanted us to work with was a security company who did great work. I was happy with their knowledge and professionalism and believe they did a great job on both of my locations. They traveled throughout the region doing installations for many different companies. Since I was the one that paid them and formed a working relationship with them while they wired the store and installed the security systems and cameras, I believed that we had a mutually beneficial relationship.

They happened to stop at my restaurant once when they were in the area for a different installation for someone else. This was a few years after the installation of my system. Soon after they stopped in my location, I received a call from the franchisor about a metal strip being off of the commercial oven, which was visible from the dining room. The strip was being replaced since it no longer had any adhesive on it. It was basically just a finishing strip to make an edge look nicer. I found the situation very frustrating that the subcontractor "reported" back to the franchisor that we had an "issue." He could have asked us what was going on but instead the subcontractor chose to "tattle" to the franchisor and made my life more difficult. It was a violation of trust.

⚜ ⚜ ⚜

Finding the right vendors.

Finding the right vendors to supply products and services can easily save you time and money. Franchisors usually have a list of approved vendors that you can work with or perhaps chose from two or three. Some services will be location specific and you will have to find your own such as an accountant, lawyer, cleaning service, grease trap sanitation service, plumber, electrician, etc.

When choosing a vendor, you must read the fine print of any contract. What often happens is that you "click" with a certain salesperson from the vendor, feel you can trust them and sign off to receive their services. Fast forward to a later time and that salesperson is no longer there and all the "deals" he offered you are gone as well. That means that any agreement you signed supersedes any deals you received.

Some vendors that regularly visit your site such as cleaning services may become lazy if you do not let them know that you are continually checking up on them. They may not even realize they are cutting corners but if you don't occasionally show them you inspect their work, they may think you don't really care about their performance. Other vendors may outright try to skimp on what they provide so they save money. It is up to you to be vigilant and not let this happen. This is one of those areas that can be extremely frustrating because it is common sense that if you pay for a service, you should receive the service. It just doesn't always happen that way.

Make sure you get any deals or promises in writing and if the vendor won't put it in writing then steer away from it. Find out whom you should complain to if you're dissatisfied. Get to know their personnel. Even though you are doing business, if you treat a vendor with gratitude and thanks for the job they do, you are more likely to see positive repeat performances.

What happens if the company is bought out or dissolves? Does the contract say that the vendor can assign your agreement to whoever is the new owner? You may not want that to happen. Does your agreement allow the vendor to subcontract to someone else? You may not want someone you don't know providing an essential service.

Since most utility companies make you put down a large deposit for their services if you are a new business, they will have to estimate your usage and may require several months worth of billing as a deposit. A restaurant may have to put down several thousand dollars, which is money you can't touch for the life of your business and who knows what other restaurants they are basing your estimated usage upon. It may or may not be similar to yours. You may be able to buy a bond instead of paying the deposit, but the cost of the bond may be almost as much as the deposit. Some companies buy gas or electricity from the utility company and then sell it back to businesses at a discounted rate. This can be a cost savings for you or it can be a pain. You should investigate any of these deals with a fine tooth comb.

⚜ ⚜ ⚜

Let me tell you more…

Since we had a baker who worked during the night, the fresh baked bread cooled on large enameled racks, which were wheeled into place for the display of the products in the bakery area. We also had a cleaner who worked during the night who cleaned the entire restaurant. An outside company employed him.

One morning, an opening manager found a baguette with what appeared to be a bite taken out of it. Everyone was confounded but since we had cameras throughout the store, it was a matter of checking the computer to review what happened. We were extremely surprised to see the night cleaner go over to the rack and pull off a piece of bread and cram it into his mouth. I called the owner of the company and told him what happened. He absolutely denied that his cleaner would do such a thing. I asked the owner to come in and showed him the video. He was dumbfounded. I even asked him if his cleaner was hungry and if he needed to eat during the night. The owner said that he would never give him that kind of privilege now and although he did not fire him, gave him disciplinary action.

⚜ ⚜ ⚜

End of Month Totals By Supplier

	Supplier 1	Supplier 2	Supplier 3	Totals by items
Breads	3329.42	0.00	0.00	3329.42
Pastries & Croissants	1439.46	0.00	0.00	1439.46
Bagels	1059.68	0.00	0.00	1059.68
Cookies	673.52	0.00	0.00	673.52
Desserts & Chz Cakes	125.51	0.00	0.00	125.51
Muffins	1092.48	0.00	0.00	1092.48
Fillings & Toppings	1090.50	0.00	0.00	1090.50
Soups	3778.16	0.00	0.00	3778.16
Dairy	1928.23	591.78	559.17	3079.18
Meats	4437.90	1203.40	0.00	5641.30
Produce	0.00	315.25	3051.01	3366.26
Dressings	330.90	0.00	0.00	330.90
Condiments	306.34	698.36	0.00	1004.70
Seasoning & Spices	36.68	0.00	0.00	36.68
Chips	882.10	0.00	0.00	882.10
Coffee, Teas & Syrups	1379.45	0.00	0.00	1379.45
Soda & Bottled Drinks	1566.12	191.39	0.00	1757.51
Smoothies	491.07	0.00	0.00	491.07
Food Other	598.47	70.62	0.00	669.09
Catering Food	0.00	0.00	0.00	0.00
Total Food by co.	24545.99	3070.80	3610.18	31226.97

				Totals
Total Food	24545.99	3070.80	3610.18	31226.97
Paper	3127.82	28.67	0.00	3156.49
Chemicals	1059.39	89.93	0.00	1149.32
Total by companies	28733.20	3189.40	3610.18	35532.78

Food Cost %	
Net Sales	94482.00
Usage $	28942.92
Food Cost %	30.63

Paper Cost %	
Net Sales	94482.00
Total Paper $	3156.49
Paper Cost %	3.34

Hobby or business.

Any person that is not prepared to handle complaints in their business is really just having a hobby. Being in business means getting complaints. You cannot please everyone all the time. All employees should be educated in handling complaints, even being able to determine when it is time to refer the complaint higher up in the organization.

A business owner not only needs to keep their customers happy, they also need to protect their employees from abuse. Even an upset customer has a responsibility to lodge their complaint in a civilized way. There are a lot of angry people in the world, and you don't want them in your place of business if you can help it.

When faced with an upset customer it is important to truly listen to their complaint. Listen and then repeat back to them what they said to show you are listening and understand. Ask questions for clarification. Let them know what you are willing to do to solve their issue and get their agreement that it will indeed solve it. Some customers will have their own idea of what they want, some just want to blow off steam and others will want to take advantage.

The majority of upset customers just want to feel that they have received a fair value for their money. So, offer to refund or replace what they have purchased with an apology for their trouble. Some customers will need a bigger apology. Know ahead of time, if possible, just how far you will go to make a customer happy. Customers that ask for something you consider ridiculous may make you angry but you still need to see *if* you can satisfy them. If not, be prepared for any repercussions that come your way. A dissatisfied customer may tell everyone he knows just how unfairly he was treated, whether it is right or wrong.

Above all else, do what you promise. If you are going to mail them a gift card, get it out in the mail immediately. Follow up, take their phone number if they are willing to give it to you, and call them to see if you have solved their problem.

Customer service.

Anytime you deal with the general public, you will some find people that will not be satisfied with anything you offer them or whatever you do for them. It's human nature. The trick is to try to appease them as much as possible without hurting yourself. You will find a wide range of perceptions of what constitutes good customer service. Many customers love to be called by their name and remembered from visit to visit. Others want to be left alone and not engaged in conversation. It is up to you and your employees to be sensitive to just what your customer prefers.

You will often find that if a customer starts to yell or curse at an employee, the other customers will sympathize with your business and your employees. I often found other customers came up to me after witnessing such a situation and they let me know that they saw the disgruntled customer being very unfair to the employees or the business.

Since many people are going through difficult times in their personal life, they often have less patience or just may be angry at the world. Venting through complaining at a business or about their perceived lack of good service is common. Some people just want things for free and it is a judgment call just how much making them pleased is worth it to you.

Managers need to have enough discretion in what they are able to do for a customer whether it be giving them their business card with a free product written on the back of the card for the next time they visit, or giving them their money back.

I have read that people will attack when they feel deprived and this has been proven true in my experience. In any restaurant, especially in an environment where you have to estimate demand and cook or bake a product accordingly, there will always be those times when you predicted incorrectly and a product will be out of stock. For some reason, the multi-grain bagels that we offered inspired a strong sense of loyalty. Although there were numerous other kinds, when someone was deprived of a multi-grain bagel, they often got extremely angry and sometimes made a scene.

You can never estimate just *how* upset a customer can get from something you feel is minor but you still have to have a policy in place to deal with it. Sometimes, it's about offering them a rain check for a free product or perhaps giving them a free cup of coffee, however, any other customers that witness the disgruntled customer's behavior and perceived "reward" has just learned that complaining helps someone get a free product. It is a balance as to keeping a customer happy and also not rewarding nasty behavior.

Some customers insist that they be special to the point that if they don't complain at least once every visit they think they have not won all they can. We had a customer that purchased our catering and every single time we worked with her, she had to find something wrong, no matter if she got a free item, got extra, or was allowed to have exceptions or discounts. It's very difficult to work with someone who you know will never be satisfied. It's more of a power thing with them and not just about satisfaction. Of course, you always have the right to refuse service to anyone, but if you do, you don't know how many people will hear about it and not necessarily the version of events you want broadcast.

⚜ ⚜ ⚜

Let me tell you more…

I had several Spanish-speaking employees. An older man, a customer, used to make sure to make comments specifically to the Hispanic workers, in Spanish. It was easily observable that at times he made them uncomfortable. I asked them what was going on and if the customer had insulted them. They looked even more uncomfortable but wouldn't tell me anything. Finally, a bilingual manager took each one aside and asked for an explanation. He found out that the customer was insulting other non-Hispanic managers and even myself in an extremely foul way, using slang words that are never acceptable. The next time the customer came into the store, we took him aside and told him he was never allowed back into our restaurant although he denied everything. The man got some type of sick pleasure in doing what he did but we didn't have to deal with it again.

With a different issue, one day I was notified that a customer was giving all the staff a problem. The female customer asked for a detailed list of every ingredient in our products, which we freely gave her. We kept a large binder full of every product in our restaurant broken down by ingredient. The book was mainly kept for the benefit of those with allergies. She became increasingly upset and angry when she didn't find anything that worked for her. She upset the person waiting on her and then upset a manager until it was my turn.

I asked her what she needed instead of just informing her of the ingredients. She gradually told me that she had just been diagnosed with breast cancer and there was a list of things she wasn't supposed to eat, including any soy. After she finally told me why she was so frustrated and upset (she had been upset for at least thirty minutes by that time) we worked together to find something she could eat. We even sat down together and discussed it. She went from being very unhappy to being very happy.

It was also a lesson for me to look at every customer in our restaurant and realize that they may have some very real problem to deal with and that being upset may really have nothing to do with us, but we could still show compassion and not take it personally.

On a positive note, on a sunny afternoon, a woman in her eighties walked into my store and made her purchase. She went out to her car and then came back in because she couldn't find her car keys. We weren't very busy so several employees walked the parking lot, the interior of the restaurant and looked everywhere, including pulling out the trash from the trash cans. We couldn't find them anywhere. She had no one she could call right then and told me that she kept another set of car keys at home and could get in the house with her garage door opener. She also told me she had just relocated here to be closer to her daughter since her husband had recently died. She was alone in a new town. I offered to drive her to her home about two miles away and then she got her keys and came back to get her car. She was profoundly grateful and afterwards came in to dine almost daily. All the employees got to know her and adopted her as their honorary grandmother. Her daughter came in later to thank me with a bottle of wine. She was a wonderful and loyal customer, always polite and nice to everyone.

The missing keys? They were discovered in her eyeglass case in her purse. Although she had dumped everything out, since they were hidden in the case, no one saw them. She had put them there mistakenly.

⚜ ⚜ ⚜

Customer Service

Courtesy

Make eye contact

Hold the door for the customer

No slang/ off-color language

Don't walk in front of a customer

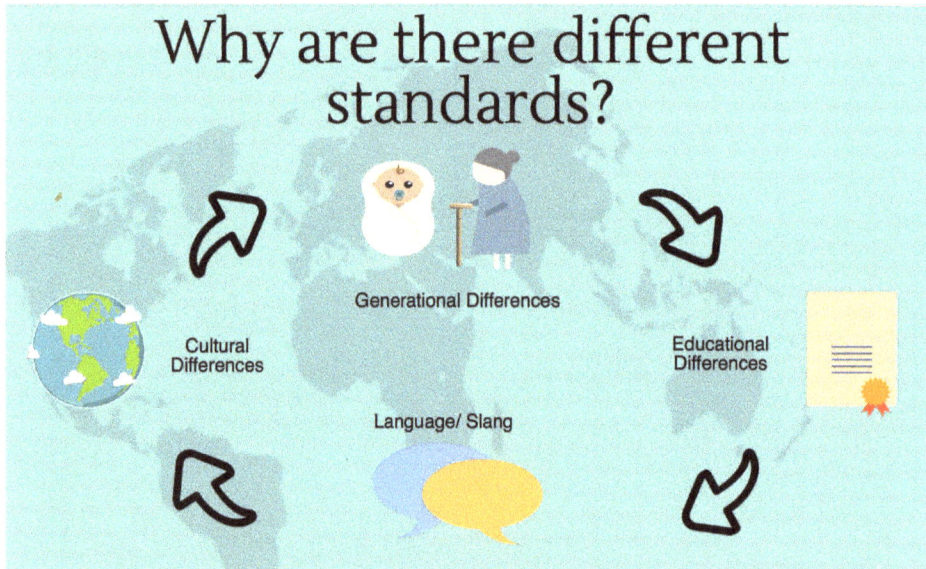

Why are there different standards?

Cultural Differences

Generational Differences

Educational Differences

Language/ Slang

Appearance

Hygiene/ Grooming

Clothing- not too tight or revealing

Exceeding health code standards

What makes a good experience?

Providing Value

Exceeding Excpectations

Friendly Service

How long to wait.

Queuing theory is that which helps you understand how long a person will wait in line to be helped or wait in line to receive their product or service. Using the time a person has to wait to your advantage can include educating them about your products, entertaining them in some way, or making their wait more pleasurable by pleasant surroundings. It also makes them feel as though the time is going by more quickly.

If you notice, car dealerships now have waiting areas that include hot coffee, television, free Wi-Fi, a desk area to do work, and some have private areas to make phone calls. The longer you make a customer wait, the more likely you have to go to some measures to make their stay acceptable and the more likely they are to leave. People are increasingly more restless and demand more.

Airports have free charging stations for electronic devices, free Wi-Fi, lots of food vendors, reading material (in stores), comfortable seats, DVDs for rent, flat screen televisions constantly broadcasting the news.

The more effort you go to, to make a customer feel appreciated, the longer they will be willing to wait to be helped.

When the customer is out for a scam.

There are always those in society that seek to take advantage of a business. A newspaper once had an article about a restaurant where a woman slipped and fell. Instead of just allowing the restaurant to take care of any medical bills, she sued them for several million dollars for pain and suffering. The woman had been known to do this to other businesses and after a lengthy court battle, the restaurant won the case. Legal fees were in the many thousands, however, without a lawyer the restaurant couldn't have fought back. Make sure you have a good relationship with a lawyer before anything like this happens. Interview several and let them know you are looking for a long-term relationship.

⚜ ⚜ ⚜

Let me tell you more....

When times get tough, people get cheap and some of your customers can exhibit behavior that is very surprising. You can't always tell who is affected by unemployment or a downturn in the stock market. I noticed in my restaurant that when people started to talk about how bad things were in the world with money being tight and unemployment numbers rising, customers seemed to try to make deals for their food, get more discounts or do unethical things.

One customer who had been a regular and coming in for several years, almost daily, always had a beverage coupon for a free or deeply discounted drink. Since the coupons were only offered periodically it was quite amazing that he had one every single visit. He told us that the "girls in his office collected them" for him, however, that still wouldn't explain the frequency. Finally, we watched him from the camera in the office one day. He went up to the cash register when no one was there and reached into the bag we kept at the side of the register for redeemed coupons. He just pulled them out of the bag. We changed our system right then and there for where we put the used coupons.

Another time, a woman wearing a heavily brocaded silk jacket that cost a fortune and driving a Cadillac Escalade, waited around the food pick up line for several minutes. We were just about to approach her to ask if she needed assistance. She saw some food she liked on the counter, ran up, grabbed the tray and ran out the side door, carrying the china and silverware along with it, got in her vehicle and took off.

I also heard a woman speaking to her companion while she waited in line to order. She told her friend that she had purchased an item from the bakery the day before and left it by mistake in the restaurant and was angry about it. When she got to the register she tried to bargain for her food but eventually ordered and paid for it. She ate the food and then approached a manager and complained about it, stating that she should get it for free. Obviously, knowing what she said to a friend made me assume that she felt she was owed something for her own mistake, however, she still had to be treated as though she were a dissatisfied customer.

Supplying free water cups so that customers can serve themselves water often resulted in the customer filling their cup with un-purchased soda or tea. We found that going up to them and apologizing that the cashier did not give them the proper cup and letting them know the unsuspecting cashier would be disciplined usually brought about a sheepish confession.

Our franchise had a policy of offering free samples. It was one of the best ways to get people to try new foods and we usually had a try of baked goods cut into bite sized pieces on the counter. Once in a while, someone would bring a plate over and load it up with the entire tray of samples and take it back to their seat. That's a very delicate situation to handle. Unless you have a sign that says, "one to a customer, please," then you have to choose whether to politely suggest that the samples are to be shared by everyone. You can create a lot of animosity when calling someone out like that but it is definitely a judgment call.

⚜ ⚜ ⚜

The best in technology.

Technology in a business is a double-edged sword. While great for helping a business be more efficient, employees will also be dependent on cell phones for communication including texting and computers. Policies should account for this. If you don't want an employee ignoring a customer or looking as if they don't care, then make a "no cell phone" policy when working. Texting and Social Media are constant distractions, especially with young people.

If employees need to receive phone calls at work (emergencies happen) then make sure that there is a main number to call and all employees know it and can give it to their family. Set a policy that employees do not converse while at work unless it IS an emergency or close to it. They should not use their own phones while on the job. It is too tempting to check messages or texts.

Anyone with access to your computers puts you at risk of accessing Internet sites that can infect your computer with a virus or Trojan. This can destroy your data and be costly to repair. Computers should have extremely limited access and be monitored by security cameras. Periodically, check the browsing history of your computer to see if any unauthorized sites have been visited and by whom.

The unplanned.

There will always be unexpected events in the course of running a business. Weather issues (hurricanes, tornados, floods, snow, etc.), power outages, road construction, employee injuries, a supply truck overturned on the highway and any manner of things can prevent you from doing business for an hour or several days to weeks. How do you plan for this? What can you do to make sure that your business continues?

Most insurance companies for businesses will have an option for lost sales due to a disaster. They will not only pay for the damage to your business but also for the average sales lost. A disaster is the worst-case scenario and there are many possibilities other than that.

What if your delivery truck is late? Will you miss crucial products for your business? Do you have another franchisee close to you that you can borrow product from? How long would it take to go there and back? What would you have to do for them in return? Document the possible procedures with phone and contact information for the franchisees close to you. Talk to them ahead of time and work out a way to support each other. Keep a log of anything someone has borrowed from you and anything you have borrowed from them. Record when it was returned and who returned it and keep this for your records.

If you have a power outage, do you know who to call for assistance? Do you have emergency lighting in your business (code will require it) so that your customers will not slip and fall in the dark? Can you still do business when your credit card authorization will be down? This should be figured out ahead of time and any emergency equipment (flashlights, batteries, calculators, pencils, manual credit card sliders and credit slips, etc.) kept in easily accessible places. Trial runs should be done in the same way as people do fire drills.

Do you know what happens if the franchisor suffers a financial loss, goes out of business or files bankruptcy? Most franchises have an association that will try to handle such critical factors as continuing business with suppliers, finding other sources and dealing with the media. You should be prepared for disasters that hit not only your business but also others in your chain as well as the franchisor. If one franchise in the chain suffers a major product liability case (someone dies from using your franchise's product) your business will suffer by association.

Know at least, who to call, have a network of franchisees that you can talk to and preplan for a negative scenario. This will minimize downtime if the worst should happen.

⚜ ⚜ ⚜

Let me tell you more…

Having an employee in your building almost 24 hours a day can be a challenge since you always have to worry about them possibly getting hurt or damaging something. When you need to do maintenance or deep cleaning, there's someone you have to work around. It's much more difficult to work around someone who has a job to do too. It can also be a good thing when something goes wrong.

One evening around 10 p.m., within the first year of opening the restaurant, I received a call that there was a leak behind some equipment in the kitchen. I went over to look at it and as I was there for about twenty minutes, it was obvious that the leak was getting worse and was inside a wall. I called a plumber, and of course, you have to pay double for anyone to work at night but within an hour the plumber arrived.

He had to open up the wall and we saw that a nail had nicked a water pipe when they installed the wall. The wall was a kind of laminated board that met code for kitchen areas. The nail was embedded slighting into the pipe and over time, with water pressure, had finally worked its way out and the pipe was leaking. In this case, it was a really good thing to have caught the leak so soon or the whole place could have been flooded in the morning.

$$\maltese \quad \maltese \quad \maltese$$

Constantly learning.

Continuing education for you can include conventions, conferences, continuing education courses as well as Internet webinars or reading books. This helps you to become more efficient at managing your business as well as keeping you in the flow of current trends and maintaining an excitement about your business. No one likes to be bored, so always learn new ways to promote your business, make it more streamlined and ways to market it more cost effectively.

Educating your employees has many benefits. They will learn to work more effectively and also appreciate that you have invested in them. You can send employees to courses (always pay them for their time), assign employees to research topics and then give a report, or send them to an industry convention or training. The more an employee knows that you believe in them, the more likely they will work hard and stay long term.

Mail.

Some businesses will not have mail delivered to their door but will have to visit a location within their shopping center where there are stands of mail boxes for the tenants. Picking up the mail seems like a simple task, but it can easily be forgotten in a busy day. You may also have to pay for a post office box, which could require a daily drive. A manager or responsible employee should be assigned to getting the mail as a daily task. It usually requires a key so there should be duplicate keys kept in a safe place in case of loss.

Because of the confidentiality of some mail, it should be a *trusted* employee. You may receive important mail from credit card processors or the government and you want to be able to analyze the mail quickly and not make your business known to everyone else.

SUMMARY

As I've tried to express, there is no way you can anticipate every situation. The best that you can do is to realize that there will be times that people amaze you in a good way and those times that they amaze you in a bad way. Human nature is what it is. You can plan all you want, cover your bases, train and rehearse and still find out that nothing is perfect, there is no absolute insurance against mistakes. My intention is not to drive you away from buying a franchise if franchising is right for you. If it is in your nature to roll with the punches with enthusiasm, if you still have that fire in your belly to move forward then franchising might be the best career for you, and I wish you all the best in your new adventure!

$$\maltese \quad \maltese \quad \maltese$$

Let me tell you more...

There are those employees that will always stand out in my mind and never be forgotten. For the most part, they are good memories but there are a few doozies that kept me up at night. I am incredibly grateful for those employees that had my best interest at heart, those that worked so hard and those that made my business like a second family.

One employee worked three jobs, getting up at 3 a.m. to clean two other fine dining restaurants and then grab a few hours of sleep and show up at my restaurant and perform shift leader duties. He constantly was on the move, tidying up, cleaning, preparing and still took care of the customers expertly and with care. I hope all his efforts pay off for him.

My general manager was a tough woman with a wicked sense of humor. She was the polar opposite of my "look on the bright side" attitude and thank God for that. She kept me from spending unnecessary money and I'm sure my constant efforts to engage the managers in new ideas and training frustrated her, but she put up with them.

I remember the challenge of one manager that always saw the negative things in life but yet did a wonderful job and was great with customers. I continually tried to get him to see things in a different light but failed. He always provided comic relief, however, with his comments.

Another manager was like a never-ending source of energy, working double shifts when necessary, smart as a whip, always trying to learn new things and looking for ways to improve our systems. He owns his own business now.

When it came time to close my restaurant, I remember the women that did all the kitchen preparation in the restaurant, who had families and worked second jobs too. They were the ones that didn't want to take too much of the leftover food home, but donate to their church. Those that could have used it the most, were also the most generous to others. They are forever etched into my heart.

⚜ ⚜ ⚜

About the Author

Cynthia Readnower was the owner of two franchise restaurants in the quick casual dining segment of the industry. She was involved in the business daily and performed all the functions of accounting, marketing, human resources and operations. During her six years in the business, she sometimes learned more than she wanted to know.

She is currently an author, columnist, owner of Skinny Leopard Media, and an award winning Life Coach. She spent years in sales and marketing positions for Fortune 500 companies and received her M.B.A. from the University of Dayton. Her interests span the gamut of changing the paradigm of how business is done, drawing out the potential in all people, and using creativity in all aspects of life.

Her first book encompassed her transition from seeing her family as "boring" to accepting that many secrets and scandals had been buried deeply in the family's past and required exposure to end the cycle of mystery.

As a publisher, she enjoys helping authors create their work and seeing the project from beginning to end; the glimmer of an idea, the work to get it down on paper, hammering out the details, the finished project and the magical look on an author's face as they hold their own book for the first time.

www.ingramcontent.com/pod-product-compliance
Lightning Source LLC
Chambersburg PA
CBHW050240220326
41598CB00047B/7456